GAMBLING

WHO WINS?

GAMBLING

WHO WINS?

Marie L. Thompson

INFORMATION PLUS® COMPACT™ REFERENCE SERIES
Formerly published by Information Plus, Wylie, Texas

GALE GROUP

Detroit
New York
San Francisco
London
Boston
Woodbridge, CT

GAMBLING: WHO WINS?
Marie L. Thompson, *Author*

Rita Runchock, *Managing Editor*
Cynthia Rose, *Project Manager and Series Editor*
Kathleen Droste, *Contributing Editor*
Jason M. Everett, *Associate Editor*
Ryan McNeill, *Assistant Editor*

Kenn Zorn, *Product Design Manager*
Michelle DiMercurio, *Senior Art Director*
Michael Logusz, *Graphic Artist*

Barbara J. Yarrow, *Manager, Imaging and Multimedia Content*
Robyn V. Young, *Project Manager, Imaging and Multimedia Content*
Leitha Etheridge-Sims, Mary K. Grimes, David G. Oblender, *Image Catalogers*
Pam A. Reed, *Imaging Coordinator*
Randy Bassett, *Imaging Supervisor*
Robert Duncan and Dan Newell, *Imaging Specialists*
Christine O'Bryan, *Graphic Specialist*

Maria Franklin, *Permissions Manager*
Edna Hedblad, *Permissions Specialist*
Luann Brennan, *Technical Training Specialist*
Susan Kelsch, *Indexing Manager*
Lynne Maday, *Indexing Specialist*

Mary Beth Trimper, *Manager, Composition and Electronic Prepress*
Evi Seoud, *Assistant Manager, Composition Purchasing and Electronic Prepress*
Dorothy Maki, *Manufacturing Manager*
NeKita McKee, *Buyer*

GAMBLING: WHO WINS?

READER'S GUIDE

Gambling: Who Wins? looks at the fast-growing gambling industry in the United States today. Chapters on casinos, pari-mutuel betting, and lotteries detail the most common types of gambling. Internet gambling, Indian-run casinos, and Gamblers Anonymous are just a few of the issues covered. Chapters of pro and con arguments and the results of public opinion polls give students a balanced view of this often-controversial topic.

Written especially for middle school, ESL (English as a Second Language), and some high school students, *Gambling: Who Wins?* gives students the most current facts available on gambling today. Current data from government agencies, research institutions, and polling organizations like Gallup and Harris have been gathered into one ready reference. In a few cases, the most current information available at the time of writing may have been dated 1998 or earlier, since agencies often take several years to conduct new studies and publish the data. The facts are presented objectively, encouraging students to draw their own conclusions and develop informed opinions.

Special features include:

- **Over 25 tables, pie charts, bar graphs and other graphic displays**—newly designed for this edition, give readers a good "picture" of the data and often provide additional information. All tables and figures are fully indexed, and sources are clearly identified. Tables and figures are easily located with the convenient numbering system. For example, in Table 3.1, the "3" means it is in Chapter 3, and the "1" means it is the first table in the chapter. Similarly, Figure 3.1 is the first figure (graph or chart) in Chapter 3.

- **Section heads**—divide each chapter into well-organized sub-topics, making information easier to find. Section heads are also listed in the table of contents, allowing readers to quickly scan for the information they need, to give focus to their report or project, or simply to browse.

- **Convenient, quick definitions in the text**—may be included in parentheses immediately after words that may be difficult.

- **Words to Know**—provides definitions of special terms used in discussing gambling, as well as other useful terms, including "mean," "median," "average," and "sample."

- **Important Names and Addresses**—lists organizations and government agencies for students to contact directly, using current addresses, telephone numbers, URLs, e-mail addresses, and fax numbers.

- **Resources**—details sources of information and provides helpful advice on further study.

- **Comprehensive Index**—improved and expanded, with references to all tables and charts.

Let us hear from you!

We welcome your comments on this book and your suggestions for ways to improve the next update. If there's a topic you'd like us to include in the future, let us know. Please call 800-877-GALE (4253), fax 248-699-8062, or write to: Editor, Information Plus Compact Series, Gale Group, 27500 Drake Road, Farmington Hills, MI 48331-3535. Please visit us at http://www.galegroup.com.

ACKNOWLEDGMENTS

The editors wish to thank the copyright holders of the excerpted material included in this publication and the permissions managers of the publishing companies whose works were excerpted here for assisting us in securing reproduction rights. We are also grateful to the staffs of the Detroit Public Library, the Library of Congress, the University of Detroit Mercy Library, Wayne State University Purdy/Kresge Library Complex, and the University of Michigan Libraries for making their resources available to us. Every effort has been made to trace copyright, but if omissions have been made, please let us know.

Following is a list of the copyright holders who have granted us permission to reproduce material in this volume of Gambling: Who Wins?

Pari-Mutuel Racing, 1997. Association of Racing Commissioners International, Inc. Reproduced by permission.

The United States Gross Annual Wager, 1997. Copyright © 1997, 1998 *International Gaming and Wagering Business*. Reproduced by permission.

Social Audit: Gambling in America 1999, 2000. Gallup Organization. Reproduced by permission.

International Gaming and Wagering Business, v. 18, September, 1997; v. 20, January, 1999; v. 20, May, 1999; v. 20, August, 1999; v. 20, September, 1999. Copyright © 1997, 1999 *International Gaming and Wagering Business*. All reproduced by permission.

International Gaming and Wagering Business Supplement, August, 1997. Copyright © 1997 *International Gaming and Wagering Business*. Reproduced by permission.

State of the States: The AGA Survey of Casino Entertainment, 1999. Reproduced by permission.

CHAPTER 1
GAMBLING—AN AMERICAN TRADITION

HISTORY AND OVERVIEW

The Early Days

Gambling was very popular in North America, even before there was a United States. By the end of the 1600s, just about every large city in colonial America (English colonies before the American Revolution in 1776) had a large lottery wheel. Playing with cards or dice was very common.

George Washington liked to play cards, and Benjamin Franklin printed and sold playing cards. The British Stamp Act, which helped cause the American Revolution, put a one-shilling tax on playing cards. This angered the colonists as much as the tax on tea. In the South, betting on horse racing was very popular.

During the colonial period, lotteries were a very popular way to raise money. In England, a lottery was used to raise money to establish the colony of Virginia. The Virginia Company held a lottery to pay for a settlement at Jamestown, Virginia. In 1748, young Ben Franklin organized a lottery to pay for military supplies to defend the city of Philadelphia from attack by Indians and French soldiers.

In 1777, the Continental Congress held a $5 million lottery to pay for the Revolutionary War. Lotteries were also used to raise money to build bridges, help churches and schools, and to aid the needy. Lotteries provided money to found such famous universities as Harvard, Yale, Columbia, Princeton, and Dartmouth.

During the 1800s, Americans were known for their gambling. Visitors said it was impossible to talk with a Kentuckian without hearing the phrase, "I'll bet you!" President Andrew Jackson liked to gamble. The president after him, Martin Van Buren, bet a new suit and $40,000 that he would win his run for the presidency.

Large riverboats went up and down the Mississippi and Ohio Rivers carrying passengers or freight. Those that carried passengers almost always had a casino, where gamblers played roulette, cards, and other forms of gambling with the passengers. At the end of the Mississippi River was the city of New Orleans, a city noted for gambling. Meanwhile, New York City had approximately 6,000 gambling houses in 1850—that is, one gambling house for every 85 New Yorkers.

The Reform Movement

During the 1840s, a spirit of reformation (correction or removal of an abuse or wrong) swept across the United States. Many societies were formed to protest the use of tobacco, swearing, and even the moving of mail on Sunday. The first women's rights movement was founded, and temperance crusaders preached against drinking alcohol. During these years, the abolitionist movement to get rid of slavery became stronger.

Many reformers attacked gambling because so many lotteries were run by people who stole the money and left town. Reformers also felt that many people who bought lottery tickets could not afford them and spent the money for the tickets instead of providing for their families. As a result of these reform efforts, most states began to outlaw lotteries. By 1860, every state in the nation except Delaware, Kentucky, and Missouri had passed laws making lotteries and many other forms of gambling illegal.

This did not mean that gambling disappeared. Gambling took place openly in such cities as New York City, Chicago, and New Orleans. The police were often paid (bribed) to look the other way while illegal gambling continued. For some people, the fact that gambling was illegal made it more exciting.

The Wild, Wild West

The opening of the western part of the country during the mid-1880s gave gambling in America a second life. Far from both government control and the eastern reformers who wanted to outlaw gambling, the West became a center for gambling. Every town located near a mining camp, a railroad, or a major cattle trail had a gambling hall. Major gambling houses could easily be found in Kansas City, Dallas, Denver, and San Francisco.

The Progressive Era—A Second Period of Reform

Between 1900 and 1917, a reform-minded group of people called the "Progressives" worked very hard to stop corruption and dishonest behavior in business and government. They helped improve working and living conditions for women, children, and the poor. They also attacked practices they considered morally wrong, such as drinking and gambling. As a result, most states outlawed gambling.

By the 1920s, organized crime took over illegal gambling. Illegal gamblers were even able to fix the 1919 World Series. In this "Black Sox Scandal," the Chicago White Sox deliberately lost the series to the Cincinnati Reds to guarantee that the gamblers would win. Organized crime controlled all types of gambling, from betting on horses to wagering on sporting events to betting on numbers. The federal government sometimes tried to stop this illegal gambling but could never eliminate it.

Legal Gambling Becomes Acceptable Again

Since the 1970s, the United States has turned full circle in its attitude towards gambling. Gambling, especially lotteries, was seen as a proper way for the government to raise money. The 1980s and 1990s saw slow economic growth, cuts in federal aid to state and city governments, and increased public needs. Many desperate state and local governments were forced to look for new ways to get more money. As a result, most states turned to lotteries and horse and dog racing to raise funds.

Politicians are generally unwilling to raise taxes because they want the people to like them and keep electing them to office. Several states have therefore turned to casino gambling as a "painless" way to make money for the government. American Indian tribes have also turned to casino gambling to raise money for their reservations.

By the year 2000, fewer Americans considered gambling as a practice that might cause people to lose money needed for their families or which might attract organized crime. Instead, gambling was viewed as an opportunity for governments to raise money so taxes would not have to be increased. Furthermore, some supporters of gambling believe that, if people want to gamble, the government has no right to stop them.

GAMBLING CAN BE AN ADDICTION

For most people who bet, gambling is a form of recreation and fun. For others, however, gambling is a compulsion—a disease they cannot easily control. These people may become addicted to gambling (in the same manner that some people become addicted to alcohol or drugs), and it may take control of their behavior. Like alcoholism, the addiction may destroy their lives.

In 1997, the gambling addiction rate in Las Vegas was estimated at 6 to 8 percent, compared with about 3 percent nationwide. The New Jersey Council on Compulsive Gambling considers compulsive gambling a "hidden epidemic" (a disease that spreads rapidly and widely). In 1997, the Council received 23,606 calls on its help line, down from 26,080 calls in 1996. However, these numbers were much higher than the 14,577 people who phoned in 1993.

Statistics from 1996 showed most callers were addicted to casino games (69 percent), lotteries (47 percent), and horse racing (42 percent); many also mentioned more than one type of gambling. Forty-eight percent of callers were married, 76 percent were male, and 85 percent were white. While the average gambling debt of callers in 1996 was $31,012, the 1998 average debt was $38,000—an amount that can leave families in serious financial trouble for many years.

Gamblers Anonymous

Gamblers Anonymous offers a 12-step program, similar to Alcoholics Anonymous, to help addicted gamblers kick the habit. By early 2000, Gamblers Anonymous meetings were available at more than 1,100 locations across the nation. This number was up from 800 just a few years earlier. All members share two goals—to stop themselves from gambling and to help other compulsive gamblers to do the same.

People with a gambling addiction can reach Gamblers Anonymous by calling (213) 386-8789, or by writing to Gamblers Anonymous, International Service Office, P.O. Box 17173, Los Angeles, CA 90017. The organization will supply callers with the location of the nearest Gamblers Anonymous. All information about the caller is kept confidential—no one else will be told.

CHAPTER 2
AN OVERVIEW OF GAMBLING

DEFINITIONS OF GAMBLING WORDS

Like any subject, gambling has its own special vocabulary. In order to understand what goes on in gambling, certain terms must be understood. Here are some of those terms:

- **Gaming** is another word for gambling; putting certain amounts of money at risk with the hope of winning more.
- **Gross revenue** is the amount of money gambling operations make after paying out winnings.
- **Gross wager** is the amount of money spent on all types of legal gambling.
- **Wager** means the same as a "bet"; the amount of money "put down" on a gambling activity. For example:*The wager on the boxing match was $100. The bettor wagered $10 on the horse race.*
- **Handle** is the total amount of money bet at a particular gambling place. The daily handle at a horse racetrack is the total amount of money people bet that day at that track.
- **Pari-mutuel** betting is a betting system in which gamblers wager on competitors finishing in the first three places (such as horse or dog racing, or jai alai). Bettors wager against each other to create "odds," and the pool is then split among the winners after a percentage is taken out by the gambling facility.

- **Take-out (or take)** is the percentage of the handle taken out by the operator of a gambling facility to cover expenses. For example, the racetrack owner must pay the owner of the winning horse, operate the track, and make a profit. Taxes and fees are also taken out to pay the state government.
- **Pay-off** is the amount of money left after the take-out, which is then paid to the winning bettors.

TYPES OF LEGAL GAMBLING

There are five main types of legal gambling in the United States—bingo, lotteries, pari-mutuel betting, off-track betting, and casinos. Legal gambling can be operated by either a state or a private business. (In the United States, only governments—and not private companies—can legally operate a lottery in which people must buy a ticket in order to win.) While all legal gambling operations must follow certain federal government rules, most gambling operations are controlled by state governments.

By 1999, some form of gambling was permitted in 48 states and Washington, D.C., Puerto Rico, and the U.S. Virgin Islands. Hawaii and Utah were the only states that did not permit gambling. Utah permitted quarter horse racing but not pari-mutuel gambling.

TABLE 2.1

United States Gaming at a Glance

| | Charitable bingo | Charitable games | Card rooms | Casinos & gaming | Non-casino devices | Indian casinos | Indian bingo | Sports betting | Lottery operated games | | | | | Parimutuel wagering | | | | | | | |
									Video lottery	Keno-style games	Instant/pulltabs	Lotto games	Numbers games	Greyhound	Jai-alai	Harness	Quarterhorse	Thoroughbred	Inter-track wagering	Off-track wagering	Telephone wagering
Alabama	●						●							●		◆	■	■	●		
Alaska	●	●					●														
Arizona	●	●				●					●	●	★	●				●	●	●	●
Arkansas														●		◆		●	●		
California	●	●	●			●	●			●	●	●	●			●	●	●	●		
Colorado	●	●	●	●		●	●			■	●	●		●			●	●	●	●	
Connecticut	●	●				●	●				●	●	●		●	◆	◆	◆	●	●	●
Delaware	●	●							●		●	●	●			●		●	●		
D.C.	●	●									●	●	●								
Florida	●	●	●			●	●				●	●	●	●	●	●	■	●	●		
Georgia	●									●	●	●	●								
Hawaii																					
Idaho	●	●				☆	●				●	●	●	■			●	●	●		
Illinois	●	●	●	●							●	●	●			●	●	●	●	●	
Indiana	●	●	●	●							●	●	●			●	◆	●	●	●	
Iowa	●	●		●	●	●	●				●	●	●	●		■	●	●	●		
Kansas	●	●				●					●	●	●	●		■	●	●	●		
Kentucky	●	●									●	●	●			●	●	●	●	●	●
Louisiana	●	●		●	●	●	●				●	●	●			■	●	●	●	●	
Maine	●	●					●				●	●	●			●		■	●		
Maryland	●	●	●		●					●	●	●	●			●		●		●	◆
Massachusetts	●									●	●	●	●			●	■	●	●		
Michigan	●	●		★		●	●			●	●	●	●			●	●	●	●		
Minnesota	●	●	◆			●	●				●	●	●			●	●	●	●		
Mississippi	●	●		●		●	●														
Missouri	●	●		●			●				●	●	●			■	■	■	◆	◆	
Montana	●	●	●	▼	●	●	●	●			●	●	●			◆	●	●	●	●	
Nebraska	●	●				▲	●			●	●	●					■	●	●		
Nevada	●		●	●	●	●	●	●						■	■	■	●	●	●		
New Hampshire	●	●									●	●	●	●		●	●	●	●		
New Jersey	●	●		●							●	●	●			●		●	●		
New Mexico	●	●			★	●	●				●	●				●	●	●		
New York	●	●				●	●			●	●	●	●			●	■	●	●	●	●
North Carolina	●	●		▼		●	●														
North Dakota	●	●	●			●	●	●								■	●	●	●		
Ohio	●	●									●	●	●			●	●	●	●	◆	●
Oklahoma	●	●				☆	●									◆	●	●	●		
Oregon	●	●				●	●	●	●	●	●	●	●			●	●	●	●	●	★
Pennsylvania	●	●								■	●	●	●			●	■	●	●		
Rhode Island	●	●							●	●	●	●	●		●	■		■			
South Carolina	●				●																
South Dakota	●	●	●	●		●	●		●		●	●	●	■			●	●	■		
Tennessee	●															◆	◆	◆	◆	◆	
Texas	●	●					●				●	●	●	●			●	●	●		
Utah																	○				
Vermont	●	●									●	●	●	■		■	■		■	◆	
Virginia	●	●									●	●	●			●	●	●	●		
Washington	●	●	●	▲		▲	●			●	●	●	●			■	●	●	●	●	
West Virginia	●	●							●	●	●	●	●	●		◆	■	●	●		
Wisconsin	●	●				●	●				●	●	●			◆	◆	●	●		
Wyoming	●	●					●									◆	●	●	●		
Puerto Rico	●			●								●	●					●	●		
Virgin Islands				◆						●								●	●		

- ● Legal and operative
- ★ Implemented since June 1998
- ▲ Table games only (no slots)
- ◆ Authorized but not yet implemented
- ▼ Commercial bingo, keno, or pulltabs only
- ■ Permitted by law and previously operative
- ○ Operative but no parimutuel wagering
- ❑ Previously operative but now not permitted
- ☆ Compacts signed for non-casino gambling, such as parimutuel wagering and lotteries; however, casino games may be operating

SOURCE: Patricia A. McQueen, "North American Gaming at a Glance," *International Gaming and Wagering Business*, vol. 20, no. 9, September 1999. Copyright © 1999, *International Gaming and Wagering Business* magazine. Reproduced with permission.

Bingo is, by far, the most common form of legal gambling. It is played in 46 states, Washington, D.C., and Puerto Rico. Thirty-seven states, Washington, D.C., Puerto Rico, and the Virgin Islands have some form of lottery. Forty-three states, Puerto Rico, and the Virgin Islands permit thoroughbred horse racing, while 24 states, Puerto Rico, and the Virgin Islands allow casino gambling. (Table 2.1 shows the types of gambling permitted by the states and territories.)

A VERY BIG BUSINESS

Gambling is a very big business. In 1997, legal gambling companies earned $50.9 billion, an increase of 6.2 percent from the $47.9 billion earned in 1996. These earnings came from gamblers' losses.

In fact, in 1997, Americans lost more than six times their money gambling than they spent playing video games ($7.5 billion), going to movies ($6.2 billion), going to sports events ($6.3 billion), visiting theme parks ($7.6 billion), and buying recorded music ($12.2 billion) all added together. (See Figure 2.1.) If the total $50.9 billion lost by gamblers in 1997 were the sales income of just one company, that company would have been the eleventh largest company in the United States.

GROSS WAGERS (THE HANDLE)

In 1998, Americans bet (gross wagered—the amount of money spent on all legal gambling) $677.4 billion on legal gambling, compared to $125.8 billion in 1982. The 1998 figure was more than five times the amount gambled in 1982, or an increase of 438.7 percent. (See Table 2.2.)

Of all the money spent on gambling in the U. S. in 1998, 72 percent was wagered at casinos—mostly in Las Vegas, Nevada, and Atlantic City, New Jersey. Most of the rest was bet at games on American Indian reservations (14.7 percent) or on the lotteries (7 percent).

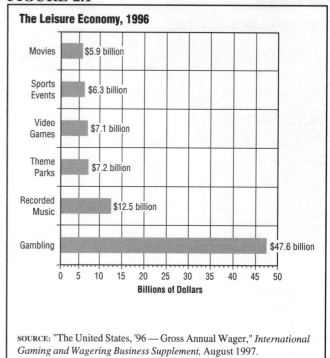

FIGURE 2.1

The Leisure Economy, 1996

Movies	$5.9 billion
Sports Events	$6.3 billion
Video Games	$7.1 billion
Theme Parks	$7.2 billion
Recorded Music	$12.5 billion
Gambling	$47.6 billion

Billions of Dollars

SOURCE: "The United States, '96 — Gross Annual Wager," *International Gaming and Wagering Business Supplement,* August 1997.

By 1998, betting on horses at the racetrack had fallen 65.2 percent from 1982, and wagering on jai alai (a game in which the players hurl a small ball against the walls of the court using a curved basket attached to one arm) tumbled 68.1 percent. (See Table 2.2.)

On the other hand, total casino betting rose 381.2 percent from 1982, and legal bookmaking grew 347.3 percent (a slight decrease from the 385 percent in 1996). Non-Nevada/New Jersey card room gambling (card games are played for money) rose 1,000.7 percent, and betting on lotteries increased 1,087.1 percent.

Gambling on American Indian reservations, which barely existed in 1982, saw more than $1.3 billion in wagers in 1990, soared to $65 billion in 1996, and rose to $99.4 billion in 1998. (See Table 2.2.)

GROSS REVENUES (THE TAKE)

Of the $677.4 billion wagered in 1998, gross revenues, or "take" (the amount of money gambling operations make after paying out winnings) was $54.4 billion, an increase from $47.6 billion in 1996 and $10.4 billion in 1982.

TABLE 2.2

Trends in Gross Wagering (Handle), 1982-1998

	1982 Gross Wagering (Handle)	1997 Gross Wagering (Handle)(Revised)	1998 Gross Wagering (Handle)	1982-1998 Increase/(Decrease) In Gross Wagering (Handle)		Average Annual Rate 1982-1998
				Dollars	**Percent**	
Pari-Mutuels						
Horses						
On-Track	$9,990,600	$3,603,200	$3,481,400	($6,509,200)	-65.15%	-(6.38%)
ITW		6,115,000	6,320,400	6,320,370	N/A	N/A
OTB	1,707,300	5,620,400	5,870,400	4,163,140	243.85%	8.02%
Total	11,697,900	15,338,600	15,672,200	3,974,310	33.97%	1.84%
Greyhounds						
On-Track	2,208,600	1,306,500	1,236,900	(971,680)	-44.00%	-(3.56%)
ITW		797,300	820,800	820,780	N/A	N/A
OTB		147,400	146,500	146,490	N/A	0.54(1)
Total	2,208,600	2,251,100	2,204,100	(4,400)	-0.20%	-0.01%
Jai Alai	622,800	212,600	198,400	(424,350)	-68.14%	-6.90%
Total Pari-Mutuels	**14,529,200**	**17,802,400**	**18,074,800**	**3,545,550**	**24.40%**	**1.37%**
Lotteries						
Video Lotteries		11,862,200	14,181,600	14,181,590	N/A	N/A
Other Games	4,088,300	34,341,700	34,350,200	30,261,910	740.21%	4.23%
Total Lotteries	**4,088,300**	**46,103,900**	**48,531,800**	**44,443,500**	**1087.09%**	**16.72%**
Casinos						
Nevada/NJ Slot Machines	14,400,000	133,895,200	137,519,100	123,119,060	854.99%	15.15%
Nevada/NJ Table Games	87,000,000	189,250,400	181,757,200	94,757,230	108.92%	4.71%
Deepwater Cruise Ships		3,437,700	3,692,100	3,692,090	N/A	N/A
Cruises-to-nowhere		3,093,000	3,884,500	3,884,510	N/A	N/A
Riverboats		115,817,800	135,505,700	135,505,730	N/A	N/A
Other Land-Based Casinos		7,932,900	7,982,600	7,982,570	N/A	N/A
Other Commercial Gambling		451,800	466,800	466,780	N/A	N/A
Non-Casino Devices		16,188,700	17,089,900	17,089,940	N/A	N/A
Total Casinos	**101,400,000**	**470,067,400**	**487,897,900**	**386,497,900**	**381.16%**	**10.32%**
Legal Bookmaking						
Sports Books	415,200	2,431,400	2,269,100	1,853,900	446.55%	11.20%
Horse Books	122,800	141,500	137,000	14,190	11.56%	0.69%
Total Bookmaking	**538,000**	**2,572,900**	**2,406,100**	**1,868,090**	**347.25%**	**9.81%**
Card Rooms	1,000,000	10,423,600	11,007,300	10,007,350	1000.73%	16.17%
Charitable Bingo	3,000,000	3,910,400	3,972,900	972,920	32.43%	1.77%
Charitable Games	1,200,000	6,034,100	6,172,900	4,972,860	414.40%	10.78%
Indian Reservations						
Class II		2,997,200	3,180,800	3,180,770	N/A	N/A
Class III		78,934,300	96,174,900	96,174,900	N/A	N/A
Total Indian Reservations		**81,931,500**	**99,355,700**	**99,355,670**	**N/A**	**N/A**
Internet Gambling		N/A	N/A	N/A	N/A	N/A
Grand Total	**$125,755,500**	**$638,846,100**	**$677,419,300**	**$551,663,800**	**438.68%**	**11.10%**

Note: Lottery handles for 1982 are for the twelve months ending June 30th
Columns may not add to totals due to rounding.

SOURCE: Eugene Martin Christiansen, "Steady Growth for Gaming," *International Gaming and Wagering Business,* vol. 20, no. 8, August 1999. Copyright © 1999, *International Gaming and Wagering Business* magazine. Reproduced with permission.

Different forms of gambling keep different percentages of the income from wagers. For example, in 1997, owners of Nevada/New Jersey table games kept 2.1 percent of all wagers, jai alai owners kept 22.8 percent, and lottery businesses kept 35.8 percent. (See Table 2.3.)

In 1997, most of the money made from gambling was by casinos and lottery businesses. Casinos kept 4.4 percent of monies bet to earn more than $20.5 billion, or 40 percent of the entire gambling market. Lotteries (including video lotteries) kept 35.8 percent of monies gambled

TABLE 2.3

1997 Gross Gambling Revenues by Industry

	% Kept	1997 Gross Revenues
Parimutuel		
Horse Total	21.2%	$3,251,400
Greyhound Total	22.3%	509,400
Jai Alai Total	22.8%	50,100
TOTAL PARIMUTUEL	**21.3%**	**$3,811,000**
Lotteries		
Video Lotteries	9.3%	1,101,900
Traditional Games	44.9%	15,464,900
TOTAL LOTTERIES	**35.8%**	**$16,566,800**
Casinos		
Nevada/NJ Slot Machines	5.7%	7,611,000
Nevada/NJ Table Games	2.1%	3,913,400
Deepwater Cruise Ships	7.1%	244,100
Cruises-to-nowhere	7.1%	219,600
Riverboats	5.3%	6,170,500
Other Land-Based Casinos	6.0%	474,500
Other Commercial Gambling	34.9%	157,500
Non-Casino Devices	10.7%	1,737,000
TOTAL CASINOS	**4.4%**	**$10,527,600**
Legal Bookmaking		
Sports Books	3.7%	89,700
HORSE BOOKS	**4.6%**	**6,600**
TOTAL BOOKMAKING	**3.7%**	**$96,300**
Card Rooms	6.7%	700,200
Charitable Bingo	24.5%	956,900
Charitable Games	25.9%	1,562,200
Indian Reservations		
Class II		899,200
Class III	7.5%	5,779,300
TOTAL INDIAN RESERVATIONS	**8.3%**	**$6,678,500**
GRAND TOTAL	**8.0%**	**$50,899,300**

Note: Columns may not add to totals due to rounding.

Christiansen/Cummings Associates, Inc.

SOURCE: Eugene Martin Christiansen et al., "A New Entitlement," *The United States Gross Annual Wager — 1997.* Copyright © 1998, *International Gaming and Wagering Business* magazine. Reproduced with permission.

on them, earning $16.6 billion, or 32.5 percent of the gambling market. (See Table 2.3.)

Trends in Gross Revenues

As shown in Table 2.2, total gross wagering for most forms of gambling increased from 1982 through 1998. Table 2.4 shows that gross revenues also rose—from $10.4 billion in 1982 to $54.4 billion in 1998. From 1982 through 1998, the greatest increases in gross revenues were in non-Nevada/New Jersey card rooms (from $50 million to $739.4 million), lotteries (from $2.2 billion to $16.7 billion), and casinos (from $4.2 billion to $22.3 billion).

On the other hand, between 1982 and 1998, revenues from total pari-mutuel betting barely increased (from $2.8 billion to $3.8 billion), jai alai revenues actually dropped (from $112 million to $45.2 million), and on-track betting on horse races dropped drastically (from $18 million to minus $5.8 million). (See Table 2.4.) Profits in pari-mutuel betting came from off-track betting and simulcasting during this period.

The makeup of the gambling market has changed dramatically since 1982, when pari-mutuel betting on horses, dogs, and jai alai accounted for 1 of every 4 dollars earned. In 1996, this dropped to 1 in 12 dollars and in 1997 to barely 1 in 14 dollars. Also in 1982, gambling on American Indian reservations played no role in the market. By 1996, it earned 1 in 9 gambling dollars and rose to 1 in 8 dollars in 1997.

In 1982, lotteries earned about one-fifth of total gambling revenues and by 1997 made more than one-third. Casinos earned about 2 in 5 gambling dollars during both 1982 and 1997. Lotteries, casinos, and American Indian gambling have all helped drive the huge increase in gambling in the United States. Pari-mutuel gambling has not done so.

ILLEGAL GAMBLING

Illegal gambling, like legal gambling, is deeply rooted in American society. Most illegal gambling involves horse racing or sporting events, such as football and basketball games. Because it is done secretly, no public records are kept and it is difficult to know just how much money is bet illegally each year.

International Gaming & Wagering Business, the monthly magazine which reports news of the gambling industry and gathers many statistics on gambling, has stopped estimating (or guessing) how much money is bet illegally. The editors of the magazine believe there is too little information to make such estimates. However, they think that, in 1989,

TABLE 2.4

Trends in Gross Revenues (Consumer Spending)

	1982 Gross Revenues (Spending)	1997 Gross Revenues (Spending)(Revised)	1998 Gross Revenues (Spending)
Pari-Mutuels			
Horse Total	$2,250,000,000	$3,245,000,000	$3,306,800,000
Greyhound Total	430,000,000	506,000,000	493,700,000
Jai Alai Total	112,000,000	48,400,000	45,200,000
Total Pari-Mutuels	2,792,000,000	3,799,300,000	3,845,700,000
Lotteries			
Video Lotteries		1,102,700,000	1,281,600,000
Other Games	2,170,000,000	15,394,900,000	15,398,600,000
Total Lotteries	2,170,000,000	16,497,600,000	16,680,200,000
Casinos			
Nevada/NJ Slot Machines	2,000,000,000	7,611,000,000	8,091,800,000
Nevada/NJ Table Games	2,200,000,000	3,913,800,000	3,834,600,000
Deepwater Cruise Ships		244,100,000	262,100,000
Cruises-to-nowhere		219,600,000	275,800,000
Riverboats		6,170,500,000	7,293,900,000
Other Land-Based Casinos		474,500,000	526,000,000
Other Commercial Gambling		157,500,000	162,700,000
Non-Casino Devices		1,737,000,000	1,830,000,000
Total Casinos	4,200,000,000	20,527,900,000	22,277,000,000
Legal Bookmaking			
Sports Books	7,700,000	89,700,000	77,400,000
Horse Books	18,000,000	6,600,000	(5,800,000)
Total Bookmaking	25,800,000	96,300,000	71,600,000
Card Rooms	50,000,000	700,200,000	739,400,000
Charitable Bingo	780,000,000	956,900,000	972,200,000
Charitable Games	396,000,000	1,562,200,000	1,598,100,000
Indian Reservations			
Class II		913,100,000	954,200,000
Class III		5,920,100,000	7,213,100,000
Total Indian Reservations		6,833,200,000	8,167,300,000
Internet Gambling[1]		300,000,000	651,200,000
Grand Total	**$10,413,800,000**	**$50,973,600,000**	**$54,351,600,000**

Note: Lottery handles for 1982 are for the twelve months ending June 30th Columns may not add to totals due to rounding.
(1) Since Internet gaming is international, its revenues are not included in U.S. totals

SOURCE: Eugene Martin Christiansen, "Steady Growth for Gaming," International Gaming and Wagering Business, vol. 20, no. 8, August 1999. Copyright 1999, International Gaming and Wagering Business magazine. Reproduced with permission.

Americans lost about $6.7 billion on illegal gambling, almost 22 percent of all gambling losses that year.

In 1999, the Gallup Organization, a nationwide survey group, did a survey named *Social Audits: Gambling in America 1999—A Comparison of Adults and Teenagers*. The Gallup researchers asked people if they had done any illegal gambling during the past year. Twenty-four percent of adults and 18 percent of teenagers said they had.

GAMBLING ON INDIAN RESERVATIONS

The Indian Gaming Regulatory Act of 1988 (Public Law 100-497) permits American Indian tribes to set up gambling on their reservations. Many tribes had already been holding bingo games on their reservations, but the new law gave them a chance to take legal advantage of the growing national interest in gambling. The law allowed tribes to make an agreement with the state they were in to set up gambling on their reservations, even if that kind of gambling (casinos, for instance) were illegal everywhere else in the same state. By July 1999, according to the Bureau of Indian Affairs, 160 tribes in 24 states had agreements allowing casino gambling. This was an increase from 147 tribes in 24 states in December 1997 and up dramatically from 62 tribes in 18 states in 1993.

The amount of money bet at Indian reservations rose from nothing in 1982 to an estimated $99.4 billion in 1998. (See Table 2.2.) The reservations kept about 8 percent of the handle—or approximately $8.2 billion—in 1998. (See Table 2.4.) These numbers are expected to continue increasing over the next few years, although perhaps not as dramatically.

SPORTS GAMBLING

Gambling on sports is legal and operating in Montana, Nevada, North Dakota, and Oregon. It is also legal, but not operative, in Delaware. Sports betting is also legal in a number of locations in Baja California, Mexico, which borders California. Almost all the money wagered legally on sports is bet in Nevada. In 1997, $2.4 billion was wagered on sports, with about $89.7 million (or 3.7 percent) kept as take-out by the gambling houses. (See Table 2.3.) This is a much lower take-out than the 5.7 percent take in 1994.

GAMBLING ON THE INTERNET

According to the National Gambling Impact Study Commission, on-line (or Internet) betting will totally change the way Americans gamble because it allows people to gamble 24 hours a day from their homes.

In 1998, there were an estimated 800 to 1,000 gambling sites on the Internet (up from about 500 sites just one year earlier). These sites have millions of potential customers. Christiansen/Cummings Associates, Inc., a consulting and financial services firm, believes the number of people who used the Internet to gamble rose from 6.9 million in 1997 to 14.5 million in 1998. It also estimated the gambling revenues rose from $300 million in 1997 to $651 million in 1998. The firm predicted these revenues would reach $2.3 billion by the year 2001. (See Table 2.5.)

Technically, Internet gambling was still illegal in early 2000. The most widely used federal law prohibiting gambling was the Wire Communications Act of 1961. This law made it illegal to use wire communications to place bets or wagers. However, because the law was written in 1961 when there was no Internet technology, some people say this law only means gambling by telephone. But because the law does not ac-

TABLE 2.5

Estimated Worldwide Internet Gambling Revenues ($ in millions)

	1997	1998	1999	2000	2001
Adult home users (in millions)	46	81	121	145	159
% users conducting on-line transactions	15%	18%	21%	24%	27%
Potential Internet gamblers (in millions)	6.9	14.5	25.4	34.8	43
Per-capita expenditure	$146	$154	$155	$16	$16
Potential Internet gambling revenues	$1,009	$2,182	$3,933	$5,555	$7,080
Estimated actual Internet gambling revenues	$300	$651	$811	$1,520	$2,330

SOURCE: Sebastian Sinclair, "Legitimacy Fuels Internet Gaming Growth," *International Gaming and Wagering Business,* vol. 20, no. 1, January 1999. Copyright © 1999, *International Gaming and Wagering Business* magazine. Reproduced with permission.

tually state "telephone communication," other people say it includes all types of wire communications.

While gambling facilities were fighting legal and political battles to legalize Internet gambling, certain states regulated or banned it. Illinois, Louisiana, Nevada, and Texas introduced or passed laws making it illegal, while Florida, working with Western Union, tried to stop money transfer services of 40 offshore sports bookmakers.

However, the Internet is an international medium. In 1999, 25 countries legalized Internet gambling, and American laws cannot control Internet activities that come from other countries. Since sports betting is illegal in most of the United States, many bookmakers moved their base of operations to islands in the Caribbean and Central America, using the Internet to set odds and make wagers. Money is transferred to an account by wire (Western Union), cashier's check, or credit card. These Internet bookmakers are taking in 1 to 5 percent of the estimated $100 billion bet illegally in the United States on sports each year. Many are also offering on-line casinos with interactive games of poker, blackjack, and slot machines.

CHAPTER 3
PARI-MUTUEL BETTING—HORSES, DOGS, AND JAI ALAI

SOME DEFINITIONS

- **Off-Track Betting (OTB)** means that a person places a bet on a horse or dog race at a location other than the track where the race actually takes place. In 1970, New York became the first state to pass a law allowing off-track betting. New York City opened the first off-track betting parlor in 1971. OTB bets are usually placed at a track branch office or a betting shop or parlor. Some states permit the bettor to call in his or her bet over the telephone. Ten states (California, Connecticut, Illinois, Kentucky, Louisiana, New York, Oregon, Pennsylvania, Washington, and Wyoming) permit off-track betting.

- **Inter-Track Wagering (ITW)** is the showing of a race on television at a site away from the actual racetrack. The person watching may bet on the race as if he or she were at the actual track where the race is being run. In the case of ITW, the racetrack has been opened solely for the purpose of showing these televised races.

- **Simulcasting** is similar to ITW. It is the showing of a race on television at a site away from the actual racetrack where the race is being held. However, the actual racetrack is also open to bettors at the track and is not open solely for the purpose of televising races. The money earned from off-track betting is divided among the racetrack owners, the OTB operators, and the state and local governments.

HOW PARI-MUTUEL BETTING WORKS

In pari-mutuel betting, bettors try to pick which horse or dog will win (first place), place (second place), or show (third place). Bettors wager against each other to create "odds," and the pool is then split among the winners after a percentage is taken out by the gambling facility.

Pari-mutuel betting also includes jai alai, a game in which players use baskets strapped to their arms to catch and throw a hard ball against three walls and the floor of a court called a fronton. The jai alai handle (amount of money bet by all bettors) is very small in comparison to other pari-mutuel betting.

The money that is bet is collected. A percentage of the money is taken out to pay taxes, the purses (the prizes that go to the winning jai alai players and owners of the winning horses or dogs), and the track. The rest of the money is paid back to the bettors who have picked the winning dogs or horses. In 1997, bettors wagered $17.8 billion on horses, dogs, and jai alai games. (See Figure 3.1 for the amount of money bet on the three types of pari-mutuel gambling in 1997.)

FIGURE 3.1

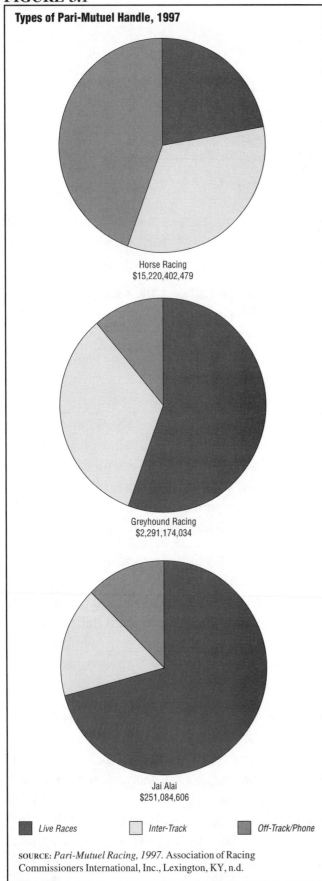

Types of Pari-Mutuel Handle, 1997

Horse Racing
$15,220,402,479

Greyhound Racing
$2,291,174,034

Jai Alai
$251,084,606

■ Live Races ☐ Inter-Track ■ Off-Track/Phone

SOURCE: *Pari-Mutuel Racing, 1997*. Association of Racing Commissioners International, Inc., Lexington, KY, n.d.

How a Person Bets

The amount a bettor makes depends on how much is bet on a given race. If the winner of the race is heavily favored (which means a lot of people think the particular horse would win), then the payoff is not very large because so many people have put a bet on the same horse.

If the winner was a "long shot," a horse few people expected to win, then the payoff will be larger. For example, if a horse is a 2-to-1 favorite, it means that for every dollar bet on that horse, $2 has been bet on all the other horses. A lot of people think this horse will win, so it is considered a favorite. If this horse wins, the winning bettors will get only about $2 back for every dollar they bet.

If people do not think the horse is very fast, and few people bet on it, it might have 30-to-1 odds. This means that for every $1 bet on this horse, $30 has been bet on all the others. A lot of people do not think this horse will win, so they are betting on other horses. If it does win, the few bettors who win will divide all the money of those who picked the other horses. The winning bettor will get about $30 for every $1 he or she bet.

The smallest amount a person can bet in pari-mutuel betting is $2. A person may bet as much as he or she likes, but the wager has to be in amounts of $2, $5, $10, $50, or $100. This means a person could bet $65 ($50+$10+$5), but not $68 or $50.55.

HOW OLD DO YOU HAVE TO BE TO GAMBLE?

Pari-mutuel racing is legal in all but six states (Alaska, Georgia, Hawaii, Mississippi, North Carolina, South Carolina) and Washington, D.C. In most states where pari-mutuel gambling is legal, a person must be at least 18 years old in order to gamble.

There are some exceptions, however. In Illinois, a 17-year-old may wager, whereas in Birmingham and Macon County in Alabama, and in Nebraska, and Wyoming, the betting age is 19 years. In Nevada, New York, and Texas, the legal age for betting is 21 years. Most states do not have an age limit for a person going to a racetrack to simply watch the horse race or dog race, although several states require that a minor come with an adult.

HORSE RACING—THE SPORT OF KINGS

Horse racing has been around for a very long time. More than 6,000 years ago, the Sumerians in the ancient Middle East ran chariot races. "Flat racing," in which the rider sits directly on the horse, took place around 3,000 years ago. The first recorded horse race took place in Greece about 600 B.C.E. Horse racing became one of the favorite pastimes of the British kings and nobles between 1100 and 1600. Because of this, it became known as the "Sport of Kings."

Horseracing was very popular in colonial America among the rich. The first race track in America was the Newmarket Course, built in 1665 in Hempstead, New York. By 1800, horse racing was common at county fairs, mainly in Maryland, Virginia, and Kentucky. The first big track with a grandstand large enough to seat thousands of people was New York's Belmont Park, which opened in 1905. In 1934, California's Santa Anita Racetrack introduced horse racing. The largest track in the United States, New York's Aqueduct, opened in 1959.

Types of Horse Racing Events

The three types of horse racing are thoroughbred, harness, and quarter horse racing. Thoroughbred racing is by far the most popular form, followed by harness and then quarter horse racing. A thoroughbred horse is taller and has longer legs than other horses. The rider, or jockey, sits on or mounts a saddle that is directly on the horse's back.

In harness racing, the rider sits in a one-horse, two-wheel carriage, called a sulky, and directs the horse around the track. The horses are trained to be trotters or pacers. A trotter runs, moving the left front and right rear legs forward almost at the same time, and then the right front and left rear legs move forward. A pacer moves both left legs forward at the same time, and then moves both right legs forward.

The quarter horse is a very swift horse that can run faster than other types of horses over a short distance. (The word *quarter* refers to the high speeds the horse can run over the first quarter mile.) The rider sits on a saddle on the horse's back. Unlike the thoroughbreds, trotters, and pacers, these strong, muscular horses can also be used for farm work and transportation.

Horse Racing Declines

NUMBER OF LIVE RACING DAYS. Racetracks are not open every day but hold "meets" over just a few days. A track might have only two meets a year, usually in the spring and fall. In 1997, there were 11,958 racing days in the United States. This was down from 13,841 in 1990. New York had the most racing days (1,330), followed by Ohio (1,229), Illinois (1,007), and California (856). South Dakota only had 13 racing days; Nevada, 9; and North Dakota, 6. Alabama, Connecticut, Rhode Island, and Wisconsin had none. (See Table 3.1.)

ATTENDANCE. In 1997, almost 42 million people went to horse racing events. This was a huge drop (34 percent) from the 63.8 million in 1990. The number of people attending racetracks in California tumbled from 13.7 million in 1990 to 11 million in 1997. In New York, the number dropped from about 7 million 3.4 million.

Thoroughbred racing was the most popular event in 1997, with a total attendance of 28.8 million people. Harness racing attracted approximately 8.9 million, and quarter horse events drew 1.1 million people.

TABLE 3.1

Live Racing Days

	Total		Total
Alabama		Montana	54
Arizona	284	Nebraska	117
Arkansas	60	Nevada	9
California	856	New Hampshire	112
Colorado	38	New Jersey	649
Connecticut		New Mexico	214
Delaware	309	New York	1,330
Florida	575	North Dakota	6
Idaho	82	Ohio	1,229
Illinois	1,007	Oklahoma	308
Indiana	142	Oregon	138
Iowa	98	Pennsylvania	790
Kansas	48	Rhode Island	
Kentucky	346	South Dakota	13
Louisiana	363	Texas	389
Maine	246	Vermont	14
Maryland	411	Virginia	30
Massachusetts	258	Washington	252
Michigan	715	West Virginia	385
Minnesota	58	Wisconsin	
		Wyoming	23
		Total	**11,958**

SOURCE: *Pari-Mutuel Racing, 1997,* Association of Racing Commissioners International, Inc., Lexington, KY, n.d.

FIGURE 3.2

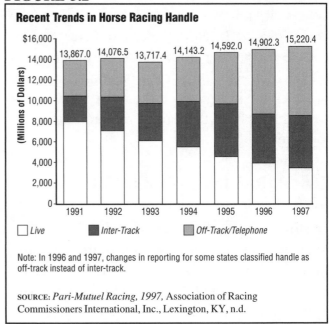

Recent Trends in Horse Racing Handle

Note: In 1996 and 1997, changes in reporting for some states classified handle as off-track instead of inter-track.

SOURCE: *Pari-Mutuel Racing, 1997,* Association of Racing Commissioners International, Inc., Lexington, KY, n.d.

According to experts in the gaming business, strong competition from other gambling activities, especially casinos, has drawn some people away from the tracks. Lotteries also offer gamblers another place to bet their money. In addition, off-track betting and simulcasting of races make it easier for people to place bets without actually going to the track where the races are being run.

The Horse Racing Handle and Where It Goes

Pari-mutuel bettors placed more than $15.2 billion in bets on the horses in 1997. New York's total pari-mutuel betting ($2.7 billion) was higher than any other state. California had the second largest handle at $2.4 billion. Both had slight decreases from 1995.

Between 1991 ($13.9 million) and 1997 ($15.2 million), the amount of money bet remained steady. (See Figure 3.2.) The average on-track bettor wagered $115.45.

In 1997, the total pari-mutuel take-out (amount kept by the track) was $3.2 billion, or 21 percent of the handle. This means that an average of 79 percent of the money wagered on pari-mutuel horse races in 1997 was returned to the bettors. The owners of the winning horses got nearly $882 million in prize money (called "the purse") for winning the races. This was down from $951 million in prize money in 1990. In most horse races, the first four horses get prize money.

The total amount of money that state and federal governments received from horse racing in 1997 was approximately $422 million. This figure has grown tremendously from 1934, when only $6 million was collected. The high point came in 1975, when the government collected more than $780 million in horse racing revenue.

DOG RACING—THE SPORT OF QUEENS

Dog racing normally refers to the racing of greyhound dogs, a lean, long-legged breed known for speed in running. Dog racing came out of a hunting sport called "coursing." A hare (a field animal like a rabbit but faster) would be released, and then a pair of greyhound dogs would be turned loose to catch the hare. Coursing was very popular when Queen Elizabeth I ruled England in the last half of the 1500s. For this reason, it became known as the "Sport of Queens."

The modern version of dog racing developed from a coursing event in South Dakota in 1904. Owen Patrick Smith, who was the host of the event, loved the sport, but he hated the killing of the hare. Smith worked for 15 years to develop a mechanical lure to which a fake hare is attached. This lure, attached to the inside rail of the racetrack, is driven around the track, and the dogs chase the false hare.

Dog Racing Declines

Like horse racing, dog racing has lost many bettors to casino gambling and other forms of gambling. In 1995, there were 55 greyhound tracks in the United States. By 1998, there were only 48 tracks open to live racing in 15 of the 17 states where dog racing was still legal. Since the mid-1990s, 14 tracks have been closed, although four of those are still open to simulcasting. Greyhound racing has been banned in Idaho, Maine, Nevada, North Carolina, Vermont, Virginia, and Washington.

During 1997, 14,557 performances were held, down from 16,110 in 1995. Thirty percent of all races were in Florida. Total attendance dropped from 30.5 million in 1991 to 14.3 million in 1997.

Greyhound Racing Handle and Government Revenues

The greyhound racing handle reached a high of $3.5 billion in 1991, but has since declined steadily. In 1997, the handle was only $2.3 bil-

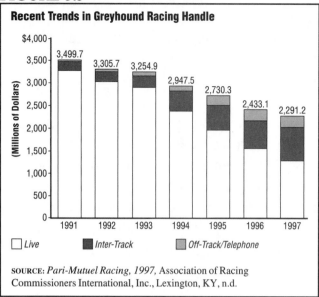

FIGURE 3.3

Recent Trends in Greyhound Racing Handle

SOURCE: *Pari-Mutuel Racing, 1997,* Association of Racing Commissioners International, Inc., Lexington, KY, n.d.

lion, due to a large decline in live track betting. At the same time, inter-track betting increased. (See Figure 3.3.)

With the handle dropping, government revenues fell from $233.7 million in 1991 to $156.8 million in 1995 and again to $113.6 in 1997. The owners of the winning dogs received $131.2 million in prize money in 1993, $115 million in 1995, and only $111.2 million in 1997.

Overall, about 82 percent of the handle is returned to the bettors, 6 percent to the government, 4 percent to purses for the winning owners, and 8 percent to the track owners for operating expenses and profit. The average bettor wagered $112.47 at the track in 1997.

Will Dog-Racing Tracks Survive?

Without simulcasting, off-track telephone betting, and permission by state governments to convert to casino games (especially slot machines), many dog tracks will not survive. Marketing attempts to make dog racing more attractive to younger gamblers have generally failed.

In addition, the animal rights' movement has been critical of greyhound racing, saying that dogs are mistreated and even killed when they cannot win. Many animal rights' activists believe the sport is barbaric and call for it to end.

This has led many track owners to improve conditions for the animals and try to find more homes for the dogs who can no longer race.

JAI ALAI

The word "jai alai" means "merry festival." Jai alai is a very fast game in which the players use large, curved baskets strapped to their arms to catch and whip a small, hard ball (made of goat hide) against three walls and the floor of a huge playing court called a fronton. The game is similar to handball or racquetball played in America.

Jai alai was invented in the 1600s by the Basques, a people who live in northern Spain and southern France. Although still a popular game in Latin America, it has seen a sharp drop in popularity in the United States and is played in only two states—Connecticut and Florida. As of 1997, six frontons were operating in Florida and one in Connecticut (in Rhode Island, where only dog racing was offered).

In 1997, an estimated 2.1 million people watched 34,436 games at 2,648 performances, down from 3,619 performances in 1990. Eighty-seven percent (1.8 million) of those who attended the games were in Florida. Total pari-mutuel handle in 1997 was $251.1 million, down from $545.5 million in 1990 and $639.2 million in 1988. Total take-out was $57.4 million.

TABLE 3.2

Jai Alai Revenue to Government 1978 – 1997

Year	Revenue	Year	Revenue
1997	$ 10,177,747	1987	$ 51,377,135
1996	11,934,999	1986	50,144,777
1995	12,960,049	1985	50,079,524
1994	21,534,496	1984	48,269,509
1993	26,585,724	1983	45,398,087
1992	30,137,047	1982	45,000,544
1991	35,031,585	1981	44,364,100
1990	38,608,321	1980	35,308,705
1989	38,898,706	1979	36,036,607
1988	43,572,178	1978	34,707,615

SOURCE: *Pari-Mutuel Racing, 1997.* Association of Racing Commissioners International, Inc., Lexington, KY, n.d.

Government revenue totaled $10.2 million—one-fifth of the $50 to $51 million it received in 1985, 1986, and 1987. (See Table 3.2.) The jai alai industry has not been doing well, and the handle has been decreasing.

Like greyhound racing, jai alai is losing out to other more popular forms of gambling. American Indian casinos have opened in the northeast, gambling cruises are offered in Florida, and lotteries have sprung up in nearly every state. In addition, jai alai suffered through a painful strike from 1988 to 1991. Without simulcasting of horse races and jai alai events at different locations, many frontons could not make a profit. Perhaps more aggressive marketing might help the jai alai industry, but its future is certainly in doubt.

CHAPTER 4
CASINO GAMBLING

A casino is any room or rooms in which gambling takes place. When most people think of casinos, they imagine the casinos in Las Vegas that they have seen on television or in the movies. For many years, casinos were legal only in Las Vegas, Nevada. In 1977, New Jersey passed a law to allow casino gambling in Atlantic City.

As state and local governments have needed more money, many have turned to gambling to raise funds. Lotteries have been the most frequently chosen form of gambling to be introduced, but 24 states have legalized casinos. Casinos can now be found in Deadwood (South Dakota) and Central City, Black Hawk, and Cripple Creek (Colorado).

Casinos also float up and down (or are stationed permanently on) the Mississippi, Missouri, and Red Rivers. They are also found on the Gulf of Mexico and the Atlantic and Pacific Oceans. Many American Indian tribes have been given legal authority to open casinos on their reservations.

First, Casinos in Nevada

Casinos have been a part of life in Nevada since the first settlers arrived in search of gold. In 1869, the Nevada legislature (law-making body) legalized gambling and, except for a few periods of reform (correction or removal of an abuse or wrong), gambling has been legal in Nevada ever since. Today, gambling is the most important business in the state.

After Nevada, New Jersey

In the late 1800s, Atlantic City, New Jersey, was one of the most famous seaside vacation spots in the United States. Thousands of tourists walked along the famous Boardwalk, a wide, wooden sidewalk-like bridge placed just above the sand.

By the 1950s, Atlantic City was no longer popular, and the local economy was depressed (there was very little money). In an effort to improve the wealth of Atlantic City, New Jersey legalized gambling in the city on June 2, 1977. All tax monies made from gambling were to be used for social programs to help the elderly and disabled.

Casino Gambling Spreads across the U.S.

During the 1980s, many state and local communities were having trouble finding enough money to operate. Raising taxes was not popular, so the governments looked for another way to collect money. Many states saw legalized casino gambling as a way to raise the needed money. The state would permit gambling and then tax the gambling earnings by taking a percentage of the money bet. The state would also charge for the licenses that the gambling casinos had to pay in order to operate within the state.

By the mid-1990s, card rooms (where players could gamble on card games) were booming in California, Oregon, Washington, and Montana. Other gamblers were betting in casinos in South Dakota and Colorado.

American Indians have also been allowed to operate casinos in the reservations. By 1999, 160 American Indian tribes in 24 states had opened casinos on their reservations. See Chapter 2 for more on gambling on reservations.

Casinos located on riverboats based in Iowa, Illinois, Mississippi, and Louisiana were opening on the Mississippi River. At sea, many cruise lines added or expanded casino operations on their ships to earn more money. Other cruise ships were simply floating gambling casinos, which sailed out into the Gulf of Mexico or the Atlantic and Pacific Oceans, travelling on international waters so that their passengers could legally gamble.

CASINO GAMES: TWO BASIC TYPES

Slot Machines

Slot machines are similar to vending machines. The player puts some coins in the slot, pulls a lever or pushes a button, and then hopes to win a lot of money from the machine. Bettors can put in as little as five cents or can try their luck on the $1 machines. Some machines even take tokens worth $100, $500, and $1,000.

Table Games

Table games include twenty-one (also known as blackjack), craps, roulette, and bingo. Not every gambling casino has every game, but the larger casinos have most of the table games.

CASINO REVENUES

In 1998, Americans bet $488 billion on casino games and slot machines (up from $438.7 billion in 1996). Most of the money was bet on table games ($181.8 billion) and slot machines ($137.5 billion) in Nevada and New Jersey.

Overall casino earnings in 1998 were a record $22.2 billion. Although more money was wagered on table games than on slot machines, casinos have earned more money from slot machines since 1983. In 1982, Nevada/New Jersey table games brought in 52 percent of all casino revenue but only 32 percent in 1998. The win from slot machines rose 280.6 percent between 1982 and 1998, while the win from table games rose only 77.9 percent. In 1998, slot machines brought in $8.1 billion and table games $3.8 billion.

NEVADA

Nevada Casinos Earn Big Money

In 1998, the 235 major casinos (those casinos that took in more than $1 million that year) in Nevada produced $13.9 billion in gross revenues. Of this, 55.8 percent ($7.7 billion) came from gambling (mostly from slot machines and table games), 16.7 percent ($2.3 billion) from room charges, 12.6 percent ($1.7 billion) from food, and 5.2 percent ($721 million) from drinks. (See Table 4.1.)

Gambling is a business, just like selling cars or corn flakes. Most Las Vegas hotels give away food, drinks, rooms, and entertainment to heavy gamblers so they will visit Las Vegas, have a good time, stay longer, and keep spending their money gambling. These free drinks, rooms, etc., are called complimentary expenses, or "comps."

Vegas Hotels Get Bigger and Bigger

Hotels in Las Vegas are getting bigger and bigger as owners try to make them more excit-

TABLE 4.1

Revenue from Casino Gambling in Nevada, 1998
235 STATEWIDE CASINOS WITH GAMING REVENUE OF $1,000,000 AND OVER

Revenue	Dollars	Percent
Gaming	$ 7,743,934,793	55.8%
Rooms	2,321,374,479	16.7%
Food	1,749,854,499	12.6%
Beverage	721,368,846	5.2%
Other	1,340,672,935	9.7%
Total Revenue	**$13,877,205,552**	**100.0%**

Based on data from: *Nevada Gaming Abstract, 1998,* State Gaming Control Board, Carson City, NV, December 1998.

ing. In 1989 and 1990, the huge, 3,000-room Mirage Hotel and the even larger 4,000-room Excalibur, the biggest hotel in the world at the time, opened in Las Vegas.

In 1993, three more gigantic hotels/casinos/tourist attractions opened—the Luxor Las Vegas, a 30-story, glass-covered pyramid; Treasure Island Resort, three 36-story towers with 2,900 rooms; and the MGM Grand Hotel, four 30-story towers with 5,005 rooms and a casino as big as four football fields.

New hotels or mega-resorts continue to be built. One example is the $350 million New York-New York, which recreates the Statue of Liberty, the skyscrapers of the New York skyline, and the Coney Island roller coaster. Another example is the $325 million Monte Carlo, which opened in 1996 and has a Victorian theme.

Recently, the Las Vegas Hilton built a 40,000-square-foot *Star Trek* entertainment area. Mirage Resorts built the Beau Rivage, a $900 million, 3,000-room resort with a 50-acre lake. Numerous downtown hotels are being upgraded, modernized, and expanded.

The competition among the casinos is very great, and each casino is trying to do something different to attract customers. The Mirage Hotel has a man-made volcano outside that erupts realistically and a huge aquarium inside filled with tropical fish, including sharks and manta rays. The Bellagio features more than a thousand fountains, with water leaping as high as 240 feet and set to dance to different types of music.

The Luxor Las Vegas contains a Sega amusement arcade. In addition, Sega is operating VirtuaLand, a virtual-reality facility of 20,000 square feet. The new Stratosphere Tower and Casino features a 70-foot mechanical gorilla and a roller coaster.

Making Las Vegas a Family Place

Las Vegas has changed its image from a place for mother and father to go alone and gamble at the slot machines or casino tables. It is now advertised as a complete experience the whole family can share.

The Excalibur looks like a medieval castle, and the hosts wear medieval costumes. The telephone operators tell the guests to "Have a royal day." An entire floor is devoted to activities appealing to children, such as midway games, a jousting exhibition, and a simulated motion theater.

The MGM Grand has an amusement park almost as big as Disneyland and a huge child care center. Parents can leave their children with an adult and go off to play the slot machines or the roulette table. Treasure Island Resort faces Buccaneer Bay, a theme park where two 90-foot ships battle every hour.

Is the New Image Working?

The new image for Las Vegas appears to be successful. In 1991, 21.3 million people visited; by 1994, 28 million people visited, and an estimated 29.6 million arrived in 1996 and 1998. Hotel occupancy rates have averaged between 85 and 90 percent.

However, hotel rooms and meals that used to be cheap because casino owners used them as a way of getting people to gamble, are going up in price because many people are going to Las Vegas simply to visit other attractions. Many casino operators are not happy with the changing situation. They feel the main reason to go to Las Vegas is to gamble and not to visit attractions. On the other hand, some operators think that people visiting other attractions are at least spending their money in Las Vegas. They also feel there is a good chance that clever casino operators can lure non-gamblers into casinos, and gambling will then become part of the fun they spend their money on.

NEW JERSEY

New Jersey permits casino gambling only in Atlantic City. The 12 casinos there grossed $4 billion in 1998, up from $3.9 billion in 1997 and

FIGURE 4.1

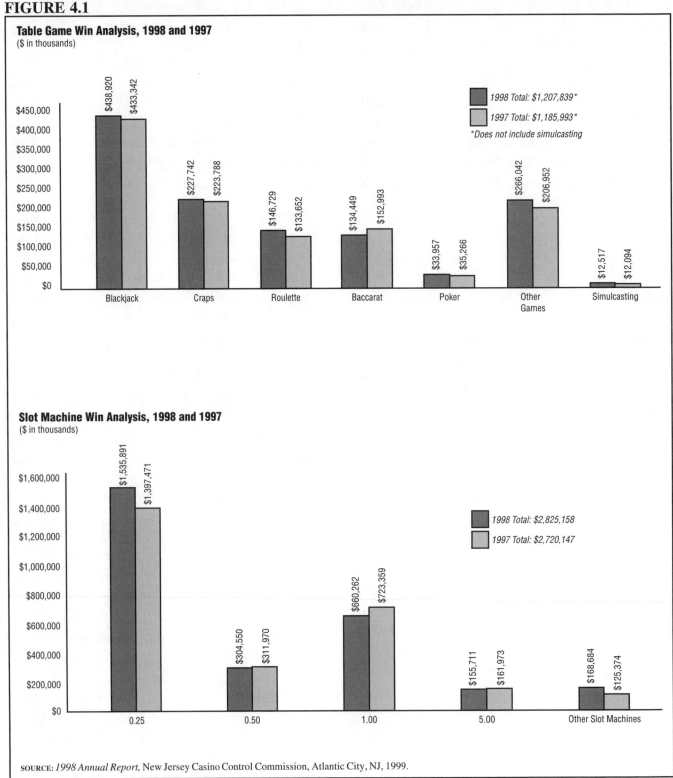

Table Game Win Analysis, 1998 and 1997
($ in thousands)

1998 Total: $1,207,839*
1997 Total: $1,185,993*
*Does not include simulcasting

Blackjack $438,920 / $433,342
Craps $227,742 / $223,788
Roulette $146,729 / $133,652
Baccarat $134,449 / $152,993
Poker $33,957 / $35,266
Other Games $266,042 / $206,952
Simulcasting $12,517 / $12,094

Slot Machine Win Analysis, 1998 and 1997
($ in thousands)

1998 Total: $2,825,158
1997 Total: $2,720,147

0.25 $1,535,891 / $1,397,471
0.50 $304,550 / $311,970
1.00 $660,262 / $723,359
5.00 $155,711 / $161,973
Other Slot Machines $168,684 / $125,374

SOURCE: *1998 Annual Report,* New Jersey Casino Control Commission, Atlantic City, NJ, 1999.

$3.2 billion in 1992. Five of the 12 facilities earned less in 1998 than in 1997. In 1998, the Trump Taj Mahal had, by far, the largest market share (13 percent) of all the hotels/casinos in Atlantic City, followed by Bally's Park Palace (11.6 percent), and Caesars (10.5 percent).

In 1998, slot machines took in the most money, with the 25-cent slots bringing in the most, followed by the $1.00 slots. Of the table games, blackjack was the most popular, with craps next and roulette third. Poker, which was introduced in 1993, brought in about $34 million in 1998. Simulcasting (showing live races on a large screen) of horse races was also added in 1993, bringing in $12.5 million in 1998. (See Figure 4.1.)

Atlantic City casinos have had some hard times. In the late 1980s, the depressed economy in the Northeast led many people to gamble less. In the early 1990s, competition from new gambling areas on the East Coast cut into the number of visitors to Atlantic City.

In 1992, the Mashantucket Pequot Indian Reservation opened a new gambling casino in Ledyard, Connecticut. The Oneida Indian Reservation opened a 90,000-square foot casino near Verona, New York, and is considering opening another in Sullivan County, just 60 miles north of New York City.

Also, many gamblers who come to Atlantic City to gamble for a few hours in one day do not stay overnight in the hotels or spend money on other things. By introducing new games and allowing 24-hour-a-day gambling, the New Jersey Casino Control Commission hopes that Atlantic City will revive and prosper. The occupancy rates at the Atlantic City hotels hit 97 percent in the third quarter of 1995. This is a good indicator that the gambling economy is becoming stronger.

A $268 million convention center has been built. Improvements to the Boardwalk, a new airport, and a new minor league baseball team should help increase the numbers of visitors. Nevertheless, Atlantic City is a regional attraction that draws most of its visitors from the East Coast. It is not the world attraction that Las Vegas is. As a result, comparisons between the two gambling centers should be made carefully.

New Jersey Casino Revenue Fund

When New Jersey legalized gambling, it set up the Casino Revenue Fund to finance programs to help New Jersey's elderly and disabled people. The 12 operating casinos are taxed 8 percent of their "win" each month. (The "win" is the amount the casinos keep after all bets have been paid but before any other expenses are taken out.) In 1998, the Fund spent $378.9 million. (See Figure 4.2.)

CASINO GAMBLING SPREADS ACROSS THE COUNTRY

South Dakota

Many states in the Midwest and West had economic problems during the 1980s and into the 1990s. They began looking for a new way to both raise money and bring tourists to their states. As a result, the voters of South Dakota approved casino gambling in the town of Deadwood, where the famous cowboy Wild Bill Hickock was killed while playing cards. Almost all of the town's gambling houses are in buildings constructed in the late 1800s or early 1900s. In fact, Deadwood is now a National Historic Landmark.

Since voters approved gambling in the town in 1990, it has become a major gambling center. Gambling promoters expected betting to be about $4 million the year it opened, but *International Gaming & Wagering Business* magazine estimated the total wagers for 1990 at about $145 million. This figure more than doubled to $330 million in 1991. Betting continued to increase through 1995 ($488.4 million), declined slightly in 1996 ($482.2 million) and 1997 ($471.8 million), then increased in 1998 ($490.4 million) and 1999 ($498.3 million).

Following Las Vegas' lead of creating family resorts instead of mere casinos, the Dunbar resort in Deadwood was completed in 1997 with 320 rooms. Among other things, it contains a fitness center, a movie theater, a bowling alley, swimming pools, tennis courts, an 18-hole golf course, and a kids' camp that is more like an adventure land.

Colorado

In Colorado, casinos have sprung up in the old, and now historic, mining towns of Central City, Black Hawk, and Cripple Creek. In the 1800s, gold and silver miners came to these

FIGURE 4.2

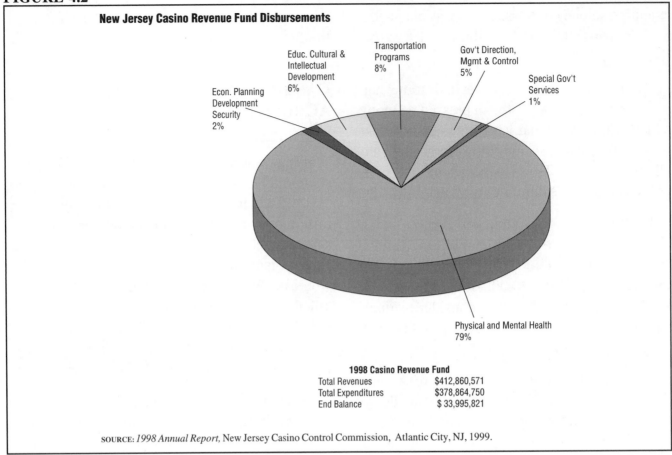

New Jersey Casino Revenue Fund Disbursements

Econ. Planning Development Security 2%

Educ. Cultural & Intellectual Development 6%

Transportation Programs 8%

Gov't Direction, Mgmt & Control 5%

Special Gov't Services 1%

Physical and Mental Health 79%

1998 Casino Revenue Fund

Total Revenues	$412,860,571
Total Expenditures	$378,864,750
End Balance	$ 33,995,821

SOURCE: *1998 Annual Report,* New Jersey Casino Control Commission, Atlantic City, NJ, 1999.

towns to mine and to gamble. There was so much betting that gamblers would set up roulette tables in the streets.

After the mining stopped, these towns almost became "ghost towns" as most people moved away. Now tens of thousands of people go there to gamble. The number of casinos peaked at 75 in September 1992 and has dropped slowly, reaching 49 in October 1998.

A person can bet as often as he or she wants to, but bets in both South Dakota and Colorado are limited to $5 each. Even so, in 1999, gamblers in Colorado's 49 casinos wagered $475 million, far more than the $244.2 million bet at 67 casinos in 1993 and the $307.6 million wagered at 61 casinos in 1994.

In Colorado, the number of gambling devices (slot machines, tables, etc.) went from 10,567 in 1993 to 13,376 in 1998. In 1998, Black Hawk had 18 casinos producing $270 million in revenues, and Central City had 11 casi-

nos making $91.9 million in revenues. Cripple Creek had 20 casinos earning $113 million in revenues. While the overall number of casinos in Colorado dropped, revenues still increased.

In 1998, the state of Colorado collected $59 million in taxes, up from only $13.5 million in 1992. About one-third (36.6 percent) went to the State General Fund, about one-fourth (28 percent) went to the State Historical Society, and most of the rest went to the three gambling towns and the counties they were in. (See Figure 4.3.) Some of this money went to restoring old, run-down buildings in these former boomtowns.

Riverboat Gambling

In the 1800s, riverboats sailed up and down the larger rivers of the United States—the Ohio, the Missouri, and the Mississippi. Almost every passenger boat had a casino, where people could spend their time gambling. Many states that are located on the Missouri or Mississippi River have brought back riverboat gambling. In 1991,

FIGURE 4.3

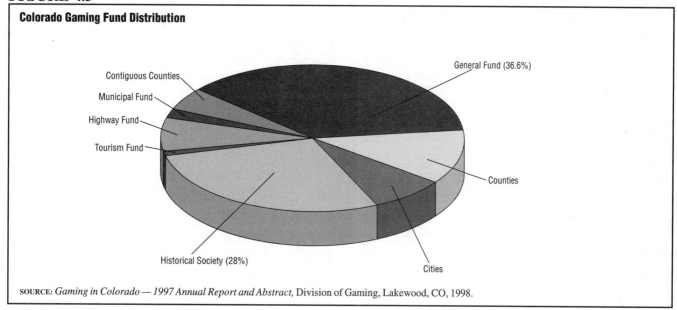

Colorado Gaming Fund Distribution

General Fund (36.6%)

Contiguous Counties

Municipal Fund

Highway Fund

Tourism Fund

Counties

Historical Society (28%)

Cities

SOURCE: *Gaming in Colorado — 1997 Annual Report and Abstract,* Division of Gaming, Lakewood, CO, 1998.

Iowa passed a law permitting riverboat gambling. Since then, five more states have permitted riverboat casinos—Missouri, Illinois, Indiana, Mississippi, and Louisiana. In 1998, 90 boats in six states earned more than $6 billion in revenue.

Most of the riverboats range in size from 200 to 300 feet long and 45 to 95 feet wide. The *President,* sailing out of Davenport, Iowa, is 300 feet long and has a 27,000-square foot casino with 700 slot machines and 30 gaming tables. The smaller *Par-A-Dice,* out of Peoria, Illinois, is 228 feet long and has 12,500 square feet of casino space with 478 slot machines and 40 tables. The *Casino Queen,* out of East St. Louis, offers 896 slot machines and 62 tables, while Harrah's *Vicksburg* has 525 slot machines and 38 tables.

Iowa and Illinois demand that the riverboats cruise on the rivers, while Missouri and Louisiana require the ships to cruise a "certain extent." Mississippi does not require the ships to sail, and many of the ships docked in Mississippi are not really capable of sailing. They are simply giant buildings constructed on barges.

Iowa and Illinois

In 1996, in Iowa, 13 boats were operating. With the removal of betting and loss limits, gambling revenues in Iowa increased sharply, from $45.5 million in 1993 to $395 million in 1996 and $496 million in 1998. Slot machines produced 81 percent of these revenues.

In 1998, in Illinois, 13.3 million people visited the state's 10 riverboats—down from $14.8 million people on 13 riverboats in 1995. Gross receipts fell from $1.2 billion in 1995 to $1.1 billion each in 1996, 1997, and 1998. In 1998, the casinos earned about $45 for every visitor. The state received $256.8 million in taxes, while the local communities got $80 million.

Missouri & Louisiana

In 1998, in Missouri, 13 ships were operating. For the fiscal year ending June 30, 1998, adjusted gross receipts totaled $898 million. About 41 million people paid admission fees to gamble on the riverboats. The state of Missouri took in $161.6 million in taxes, while local communities took in $18 million.

Louisiana approved riverboat gambling in 1991 and allows 15 boats on its 11 lakes and rivers. As of December 1998, there were 13 riverboat casinos in the state. Each parish (county) is limited to six boats, but most of them sail out of New Orleans or nearby parishes.

Many optimistic state leaders had hoped that riverboat gambling would improve Louisiana's ailing economy and perhaps transform New Orleans into the next Las Vegas. However, in 1994, two riverboats operating in New Orleans, the *Grand Palais* and the *Crescent City Queen,* closed and went bankrupt. A year later, Harrah's Jazz Co., a land-based casino, also closed.

Nevertheless, during the 1997–98 fiscal year, Louisiana casinos took in $1.27 billion and the state collected $235.3 million in taxes, mostly from gambling boats in Shreveport, Bossier City, and Lake Charles.

Mississippi

Mississippi has promoted riverboat gambling more than any other state. By the end of 1999, 30 boats were operating and revenues had increased dramatically—from $790 million in 1993 to $1.8 billion in 1997 and $2.1 billion in 1999. The state of Mississippi receives 8 percent of this total, or about $168 million. The Gulf Coast casinos in Biloxi had higher revenues than the riverboats until 1994. Since then, however, the river counties have increased revenues, while several casinos on the Gulf Coast have gone bankrupt. Development of riverboat gambling in neighboring Louisiana has caused this decline. However, the opening of quality hotels, like the Beau Rivage—a $650 million, 1,780-room hotel, casino, and marina—on Biloxi Beach, may encourage more gamblers.

Deep-Water Cruising

Gambling does not take place just on riverboats. Gamblers may board the *Pride of Galveston, LA Cruise,* and *Europa Jet,* based out of Texas and Mississippi, and take a three- to five-hour trip out into the Gulf of Mexico. Or they may travel to several Florida ports and get on one of several ships, which cruise out into international waters or sail to the Bahamas. When a ship is on international waters, gamblers can bet at the ship's casinos and slot machines until the boat returns to United States waters.

REGULAR CRUISES. Almost all major cruise ships offer gambling as entertainment for their passengers, along with shows, dining, dancing, and shuffleboard. The Carnival Cruise Lines' Ecstasy, a very large cruise ship, has 234 slot machines, 16 blackjack tables, 3 roulette wheels, 2 crap tables, and 3 poker tables. The cruise lines say that gambling is just one thing among many for people to do on cruises and is not the most important thing.

Because cruise companies want people to have a good time and leave feeling happy, most cruise ships have a loss-limit of $100 to $200 per day, so that no one will lose too much money. *International Gaming & Wagering Business* magazine reported that United States-based deep-water cruise ships earned an estimated $244 million in 1997 from their gambling operations.

CRUISES TO NOWHERE. Cruises to nowhere, or day trips, are offered from several coastal ports in Florida, Georgia, Massachusetts, New York, South Carolina, and Texas. Gambling ships travel from three to nine miles into international waters, out of the reach of state and federal laws. About 23 ships operate out of Florida, the only state where day cruises have been successful. This is most likely because the weather in Florida is pleasant most of the year, there is a large tourist base, and—as of the year 2000—the state had not legalized casinos.

Card Rooms

Card rooms are small gambling parlors where people can come to play cards, usually poker and blackjack, with other people for money. Currently, card rooms are legal in 13 states.

In August 1998, the *International Gaming and Wagering Business* magazine reported that betting in card rooms has increased tenfold from about $1 billion in 1982 to about $10.4 billion in 1997. More than 90 percent of this money was wagered in California. During the same period, revenues increased from $50 million to $700.2 million. Public card rooms have been legal in California since the Gold Rush days and, in 1999, an estimated 229 to 330 licensed gambling parlors with over 2,164 tables were operating there.

The state of Washington has more than 80 clubs and limits bets to $10 per wager. Montana has more than 50 small clubs and limits the betting to $300 per wager. North Dakota has about 20 clubs, with most of the earnings going to charity. Oregon permits "social gambling"—poker and blackjack games with small amounts of money at risk—in taverns and bars. Card rooms are also legal in Deadwood, South Dakota; in Central City, Black Hawk, and Cripple Creek, Colorado; and in Florida.

The card parlors usually earn money by charging the players for every hour or every hand they play. Card tables are also found in Nevada and Atlantic City, but they earn far less money than the slot machines or casino tables. As a result, there are only about 500 tables in all of Nevada.

A GROWING BUSINESS

In only a few years, casino gambling has spread from only two states to 14 states (the latter with some form of government approval). This does not include gambling on American Indian reservations, which brings the total number of states with legalized gambling to 24. (Gambling on reservations is covered in Chapter 2.)

Many states see gambling as a way to improve their economy and raise tax money. Many gaming business people believe there is a large demand for casino gambling—they think many Americans would go to a casino to gamble for entertainment if they were given the opportunity.

The early successes of gambling in South Dakota and Colorado, of riverboat gambling on the Mississippi and Missouri, and the increases in casino gambling on cruise ships would seem to show that they are right. According to a poll taken in 1999 by the American Gambling Association, Washington, D.C., 57 percent of adults in the United States felt that casino gambling is acceptable for themselves or others. (See Figure 4.4.)

For a portrait of the typical casino gambler, see Figure 4.5, which shows the median income, age, education, and employment of casino players. This figure also shows the median income,

FIGURE 4.4

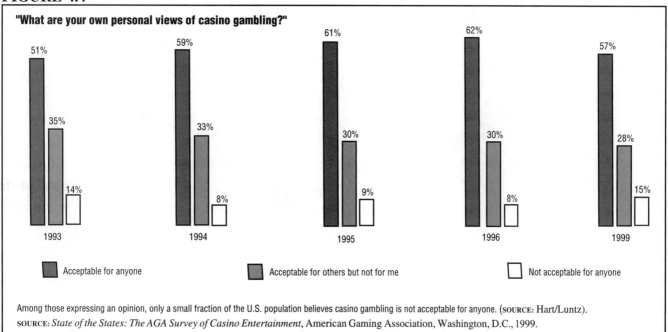

Among those expressing an opinion, only a small fraction of the U.S. population believes casino gambling is not acceptable for anyone. (SOURCE: Hart/Luntz).

SOURCE: *State of the States: The AGA Survey of Casino Entertainment*, American Gaming Association, Washington, D.C., 1999.

FIGURE 4.5

Demographic Portrait of Casino Players, 1998

Median Household Income

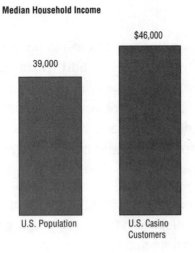

Median Age (Adults 21 and older)

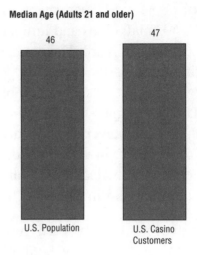

Education

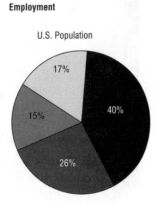

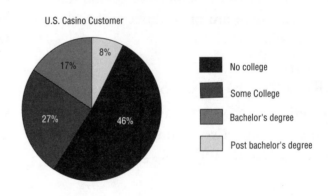

Employment

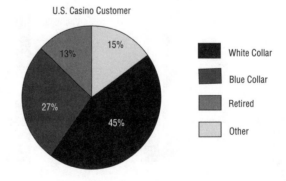

SOURCE: *State of the States: The AGA Survey of Casino Entertainment,* American Gaming Association, Washington, DC, 1999. [Harrah's Entertainment, Inc., INFO Research, Inc., U.S. Census Bureau, U.S. Bureau of Labor Statistics]

FIGURE 4.6

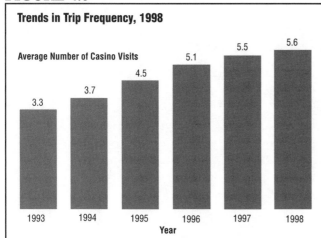

Trends in Trip Frequency, 1998

Average Number of Casino Visits

Those households visiting casinos on average took 5.6 trips to casinos in 1998, or less than once every two months.

SOURCE: *State of the States: The AGA Survey of Casino Entertainment,* American Gaming Association, Washington, D.C. 1999. [Harrah's Entertainment, Inc., INFO Research, Inc].

age, education, and employment of the total U.S. population. As shown, there is a significant difference in income between casino gamblers and the rest of the population, but very little difference in age, education, or employment.

Among American households who gambled in casinos, the frequency of visits increased from 3.3 visits per household in 1993 to 5.6 visits in 1998. (See Figure 4.6.) When all of the casino visits in the United States in 1998 are added up, and the total is divided by region, people living in the Northeast made the smallest percentage of total visits (19 percent), while people living in the North Central area made the largest percentage (30 percent). (See Figure 4.7.)

FIGURE 4.7

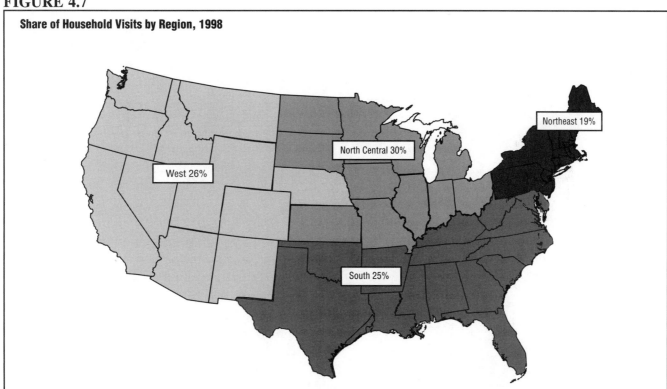

Share of Household Visits by Region, 1998

The North Central region of the United States generates the largest proportion of casino visits, while the Northeast region generates the smallest proportion.

SOURCE: *State of the States: The AGA Survey of Casino Entertainment,* American Gaming Association, Washington, D.C., 1999. [Harrah's Entertainment, Inc., INFO Research, Inc.]

CHAPTER 5
LOTTERIES

A lottery is a game in which the player buys a numbered ticket and hopes to win a prize if the number is drawn from among the tickets bought. As of 1999 lotteries were legal in 37 states, Washington, D.C., the Virgin Islands, and Puerto Rico. Lotteries are also legal in all the provinces and territories of Canada. (See Table 5.1.)

Lottery is different from other forms of gambling because it is the most widely played in the entire United States (most adults have played it). It is also the only type of gambling that is a monopoly, that is, totally controlled by the state governments.

Although state lotteries have the promise of paying out big winnings—millions and even tens of millions of dollars—they have the worst odds of all forms of gambling (about one chance in 12 to 14 million).

A PART OF AMERICAN HISTORY

Lotteries have been a part of American life since the settlement of Jamestown, Virginia, which was paid for by a lottery. Before the colonial governments (the governments in the colonies before the American Revolution) set up regular tax systems, many used lotteries to help pay for roads, schools, and universities.

Many churches were also built from money raised through lotteries. Some of the nation's most famous banks—including the Chase Manhattan Bank and the First City National Bank of New York—were founded by people who ran lotteries.

Many lotteries were not honestly run, and some lottery managers stole the money. This sort of dishonesty led many people to oppose the lotteries, and by 1840 most northern states had outlawed them. By 1860 many western and southern states had also abolished lotteries. Between 1860 and 1895 the federal government passed laws that made it impossible for lotteries to operate. Virtually no legal lotteries operated in the United States by the end of the 1800s.

NEW LOTTERIES BEGIN, 1964

In 1964 following some changes in the federal laws, the state of New Hampshire became the first state in the twentieth century to legalize lottery games. New York began a state lottery in 1967, and New Jersey followed in 1971.

In the 1980s lotteries began to spread across the country for several reasons. The federal government began requiring the state governments to pay for many of the services the federal government used to pay for. At the same time many citizens were getting upset about paying high taxes.

TABLE 5.1

United States Lottery Sales-Fiscal 1999
Unaudited Results (dollars in millions)

	Instant & Pulltabs	Lotto	5-number/ Cash Lotto	4-number Lotto (1)	Powerball	Big Game	Daily Numbers	Keno	VLTs (2)	Other	FY1999 Total Lottery Sales	FY1998 Total Lottery Sales	Percent Change
Arizona	$109.4	$48.7	$9.0		$93.7		$7.5				$268.3	$250.7	7.0%
California	959.4	1,036.1	160.6				79.7	$256.0		$9.9	2,501.7	2,294.4	9.0%
Colorado	233.9	119.7	12.1							2.7	368.4	374.3	-1.6%
Connecticut	474.0	51.3	48.4		124.6		172.7				871.0	805.6	8.1%
Delaware	20.1	10.6			73.2		45.1		$377.6	0.8	527.4	447.2	17.9%
D.C. (3)	29.4		8.7	$1.7	35.9		133.7				209.3	226.4	-7.6%
Florida	676.1	737.7	241.8				508.7			14.8	2,179.1	2,131.1	2.3%
Georgia	796.2	117.0	84.7			$199.2	777.8	59.4			2,034.3	1,736.1	17.2%
Idaho	57.9	3.2	2.1		27.3						90.5	89.6	0.9%
Illinois	568.6	168.7	113.8			193.5	479.9				1,524.4	1,577.0	-3.3%
Indiana	348.4	103.8	9.8	5.7	156.5		57.1				681.4	648.2	5.1%
Iowa	119.6		4.8	4.2	51.8		3.8				184.1	173.9	5.9%
Kansas	87.8		17.2	4.6	50.4		4.9	34.0			198.9	192.0	3.6%
Kentucky	277.8	33.8	16.7	5.1	117.7		132.0				583.1	585.0	-0.3%
Louisiana	109.7	30.1	2.6	7.0	96.8		50.1				296.2	292.9	1.1%
Maine	106.5	24.7	4.7				8.6				144.5	148.9	-2.9%
Maryland	177.0	48.2	26.3			52.4	496.0	280.3			1,080.3	1,072.6	0.7%
Massachusetts	2,165.1	128.1	53.7			96.0	376.7	538.3			3,358.0	3,199.4	5.0%
Michigan (3)	642.7	167.4	29.0			192.9	730.8	11.7			1,774.5	1,637.6	8.4%
Minnesota	265.5		19.3	6.4	85.8		13.0				390.0	372.9	4.6%
Missouri	277.8	25.0	23.5		132.7		54.4				513.3	494.3	3.9%
Montana	7.3	2.7	4.4	1.0	14.6						30.0	29.8	0.7%
Nebraska	35.1	0.3	4.8	2.2	30.0						72.4	73.8	-2.0%
New Hampshire	119.9	14.1	4.5	2.3	48.8		9.3				199.0	183.7	8.3%
New Jersey	528.3	283.4	101.9	44.2		10.9	689.4				1,658.2	1,630.3	1.7%
New Mexico	46.5		5.0	1.9	35.8						89.2	84.9	5.1%
New York	911.5	749.2	360.9				1,142.8	533.2			3,697.6	3,943.1	-6.2%
Ohio	1,128.9	421.7	69.9				524.5				2,144.9	2,195.8	-2.3%
Oregon	137.2	41.7			43.3			92.2	952.8	11.5	1,278.7	1,173.0	9.0%
Pennsylvania	448.5	243.6	209.6				767.0				1,668.7	1,668.4	0.0%
Rhode Island	51.5		5.9		52.6		28.7	57.6	545.5		741.4	634.1	16.9%
South Dakota	13.2	1.0	1.9	0.7	9.1				528.8		554.6	555.2	-0.1%
Texas (4)	1,436.8	742.7	197.0	87.2			185.6				2,649.3	3,153.4	-16.0%
Vermont	57.1	8.8	2.2				2.3				70.4	74.1	-4.9%
Virginia	337.3	121.3	32.1			79.6	355.5			8.3	934.5	914.2	2.2%
Washington	236.6	140.0	44.1	24.2			18.0	10.5			473.4	454.7	4.1%
West Virginia	79.2		6.5	1.9	81.8		16.3	16.3	741.6		943.6	704.8	33.9%
Wisconsin	230.8	21.3	31.7	7.0	101.6		35.8				428.2	418.6	2.3%
Total U.S.	$14,309.2	$5,646.1	$1,970.9	$207.4	$1,463.8	$824.5	$7,907.1	$1,889.8	$3,146.3	$48.1	$37,413.1	$36,641.9	2.1%

(1) Indicates the multistate online game, Cash4Life, and other similar four number games.
(2) Video lottery sales indicated are cash-in figures for all states except Delaware, which reports only net machine income.
(3) District of Columbia and Michigan figures are lottery estimates for the fiscal year ending 9/30/99.
(4) Texas lottery sales are for the 12 months ending July 31, 1999 (and July 31, 1998 for comparison).

Canada Lottery Sales-Fiscal 1999
(Canadian dollars, in millions)

	Instant & Pulltabs	Lotto	Spiel	3-digit	4-digit	Sports Lottery	Passive	Keno	VLTs/ Slots (1)	Other	FY 1999 Total Lottery Sales	FY 1998 Total Lottery Sales	Percent Change
Total Canada	$1980.6	$2,466.1	$472.3	$91.9	$3.0	$333.3	$116.6	$359.9	$1278.0	$0.1	$7101.8	$6545.0	8.5%

SOURCE: Patricia McQueen, *Mixed Results in North America,* International Gaming and Wagering Business, vol. 20, no. 9, September 1999.

State and local governments needed money badly. Many saw lotteries as an easy way to raise large amounts of money without upsetting the voters. Lottery promoters usually said that money earned from lotteries would be used for a good purpose, such as education or helping older people. As a result more and more states introduced lotteries.

TYPES OF LOTTERY GAMES

Instant Lottery

In instant lotteries a player buys a ticket and immediately finds out if he or she has picked a winning number. Instant tickets have a coating, which the player scratches off to uncover the number or symbol underneath. This number or symbol indicates whether or not the ticket is a "winning ticket." Every state that has legalized lotteries has an instant lottery.

Numbers—or Pick 3, Pick 4

In the numbers game a bettor puts money on a two- or three-digit number from 00 to 999. The winning numbers are determined by randomly drawn items, such as Ping-Pong balls, from a machine. In 1999, 32 states, the District of Columbia, and Puerto Rico offered numbers games.

Lotto

To play lotto, a bettor chooses any five to six numbers from a pool of 40 to 44 numbers and gambles between $1 and $4 on those numbers. Many hundreds of thousands, even millions, of people buy tickets for these lotteries. Therefore, the jackpots can be huge—often many millions of dollars. Winning numbers are drawn every week. If no one wins, the money is added to the following week's drawing, so the jackpot becomes even bigger.

POWERBALL. Powerball is a multi-state lotto game that can offer huge, multimillion dollar jackpots, usually much larger than state lottos offer. Twenty-two states (generally states with smaller populations) and the District of Columbia have combined to offer *Powerball.* Some states with their own state lottos also offer *Powerball* because they think it benefits their state games.

Video Lottery

To play video lottery (called video lottery terminals or VLTs), the player puts a quarter or dollar bill into a video game. Then the machine prints out a ticket that can be cashed in if it is a winner.

Some people are concerned about the addictive nature of video lotteries. In fact, opponents of gambling often refer to VLTs as "the crack of gambling." Because of this, VLTs have had a hard time being legalized in most states. Unlike most lottery games, in which only around 50 percent is paid back to the players, VLTs return about 90 percent. Operators of other forms of gambling fear that the popularity of VLTs will cut into their profits. In 1999 VLT sales were a major portion of all lottery sales.

VLTs have been successfully introduced in South Dakota, West Virginia, Louisiana, Oregon, Rhode Island, and Delaware. Their success has led several other states to consider legalizing VLTs.

LOTTERY SALES

Lotteries are very big business. In 1986 lotteries surpassed casino gambling for the first time as the largest type of gambling business in America. According to *International Gaming & Wagering Business* (IGWB) magazine, Americans bet $37.4 billion in 1999, up from $36.6 billion in 1998. (See Table 5.1.) Although both amounts were huge increases from the $21.8 billion gambled in 1992, they represented a great decline from the $42.8 billion bet in 1997. The IGWB thinks the decrease may be due to the lower prize money paid by the states and to more people betting on multistate games which award more money.

Due to the increased popularity of *Powerball,* Delaware saw a huge increase of 212 percent in total sales between 1997 and 1996. New Mexico increased sales by 189 percent due to the popularity of instant lotteries. West Virginia had a 54 percent increase resulting from VLT popularity. These increases slowed between 1998 and 1999 to 17.9 percent in Delaware, 5.1 percent in New Mexico, and 33.9 percent in West Virginia. In Canada lottery sales reached $7.1 billion in 1999, up 8.5 percent from 1998. (See Table 5.1.)

LOTTERY REVENUES

Lotteries keep a much higher percentage of the money bet (45.5 percent of all non-VLT bets) than any other type of gambling. For example, the horse track retains 20.5 percent; the slot machines, 6 percent; the casino tables, 2 percent; and bingo, 24.5 percent. Therefore, while lotteries make up only 7 percent of all monies bet on gambling, they bring in 35 percent of all revenues.

Where Do the Revenues Go?

Most lottery revenues go into state programs. In the beginning they helped state programs such as education. In many cases, however, instead of adding lottery revenues to their existing budgets for these programs, states cut their program budgets by the amount of lottery funds received. Thus, the net benefit to the programs becomes zero. Florida is an example of one state that did this.

On the other hand, the state of Georgia is an example of the lottery helping state programs. The Helping Outstanding Pupils Educationally program (HOPE) began in 1993. It costs about $200 million per year and is financed entirely through the state. HOPE has provided free tuition to 250,000 college students. It has bought new computers and satellite dishes for the state's public schools and improved vocational and technical schools. It has also funded new preschools for children from low-income families.

New York, Michigan, New Hampshire, and California use their monies to fund education. New Jersey helps provide homes for disabled veterans and benefits for the elderly. Pennsylvania also uses its funds to help the elderly. Oregon builds school buildings and fish ladders (which help salmon get upstream to lay their eggs). Colorado helps fund parks and recreation, while Wisconsin provides property tax relief. Massachusetts gives the money to local governments and the arts, and Arizona sets aside a special amount for transportation.

LOTTERY PRIZES

The percentage of payoff to players from lotteries is much smaller than from other forms of gambling. Nonetheless, despite the fact that the chances of winning are very small, most Americans like to play the lottery. No skill is required, the tickets do not cost very much, and they are easy to buy. Lottery tickets are sold in grocery stores, liquor stores, convenience stores, and newsstands). In addition, winnings can be huge.

A Marketing Challenge

Lotteries are directly available to about 88 percent of the nation's population. Lottery directors must keep developing new lottery games to maintain players' interest. To attract more players, lotteries have tied their games with the game Monopoly, the movie Rocky, the winning spirit of the Olympics, the singer Buddy Holly, and the soft drink 7-UP.

Most lottery players are older than 40 years of age. Lottery marketers want to attract younger players without losing the older players. Some believe the best way to attract younger adult players, especially males, is to tie the lottery to sports. On the other hand, lottery marketers must be careful not to appear to be trying to attract young people under 18 years of age. Underage gambling is illegal and encouraging those under 18 to play the lottery would cause a negative reaction from the adult population.

FIGURE 5.1

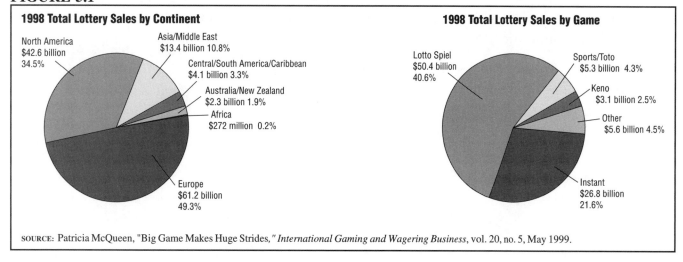

1998 Total Lottery Sales by Continent

North America
$42.6 billion
34.5%

Asia/Middle East
$13.4 billion 10.8%

Central/South America/Caribbean
$4.1 billion 3.3%

Australia/New Zealand
$2.3 billion 1.9%

Africa
$272 million 0.2%

Europe
$61.2 billion
49.3%

1998 Total Lottery Sales by Game

Lotto Spiel
$50.4 billion
40.6%

Sports/Toto
$5.3 billion 4.3%

Keno
$3.1 billion 2.5%

Other
$5.6 billion 4.5%

Instant
$26.8 billion
21.6%

SOURCE: Patricia McQueen, "Big Game Makes Huge Strides," *International Gaming and Wagering Business*, vol. 20, no. 5, May 1999.

A NATIONAL LOTTERY

Several congressmen have introduced national lottery bills, but to date, none have succeeded. Some of the major arguments in support of a national lottery are:

- It would be a voluntary method of raising money.
- Estimated revenues of $6 billion to $50 billion a year could reduce the national debt, help the Social Security system, or be used for education and child welfare programs.
- A lottery would affect everyone equally, regardless of income.
- Studies show that state-operated lotteries lower the number of people who play illegal numbers games.

Some of the major arguments against a national lottery are:

- We need better methods than a lottery to balance the federal budget.
- It would not provide enough money and would make only a small dent in the total national debt.
- It is immoral (wrong), creating the feeling that the "chance" ethic is more important than the "work" ethic.
- It promotes compulsive gambling.
- Proportionally, it takes a larger amount of money from the poor than from middle- and upper-income groups.

- It contributes to organized crime.
- A national lottery would become a direct competitor to state lotteries.

LOTTERIES—THE WHOLE WORLD PLAYS

Lotteries are as popular in other parts of the world as they are in the United States. Every continent has lotteries. In 1998 according to the *International Gaming and Wagering Business*

TABLE 5.2

Top Ten World Lottery Organizations by 1998 Sales

Rank	Lottery	Country	1998 Sales (in billions)
1	The U.K. National Lottery	U.K.	$9.1
2	Amministrazione Autonoma del Monopoli di Stato	Italy	$8.1
3	Organismo Nacional de Loterias y Apuestas	Spain	$7.0
4	La Francaise des Jeux	France	$6.1
5	Dai-Ichi Kangyo Bank Lottery	Japan	$6.0
6	New York State Lottery	U.S.	$3.9
7	Massachusetts State Lottery	U.S.	$3.2
8	Texas State Lottery	U.S.	$3.1
9	Organizacion Nacional de Ciegos de Espana	Spain	$2.6
10	Sisal Sport Italia	Italy	$2.4

Top Ten Countries by 1998 Lottery Sales

Rank	Country	1998 Sales (in billions)
1	United States	$36.7
2	Italy	$12.3
3	United Kingdom	$9.9
4	Spain	$9.7
5	Germany	$9.4
6	France	$6.1
7	Japan	$6.0
8	Canada	$5.1
9	Malaysia	$2.1

SOURCE: Patricia McQueen, "Big Game Makes Huge Strides," *International Gaming and Wagering Business,* vol. 20, no. 5, May 1999.

magazine, worldwide lottery sales (including the United States) reached $125 billion, almost double the $64.4 billion in 1990.

By continent, Europe had the most lottery sales ($61.2 billion), followed by North America ($42.8 billion), Asia/Middle East ($13.4 billion), Central/South America/Caribbean ($4.1 billion), Australia/New Zealand ($2.3 billion), and Africa ($272.8 million). (See Figure 5.1.)

By country, the United States had the most lottery sales ($36.7 billion), followed by Italy ($12.3 billion), the United Kingdom ($9.9 billion), Spain ($9.7 billion), Germany ($9.4 billion), and France ($6.1 billion). (See Table 5.2.)

CHAPTER 6
PUBLIC OPINION ABOUT GAMBLING

In 1999 the Gallup Organization surveyed 1,523 American adults over the age of 18 and 501 teenagers ages 13 to 17 regarding their attitudes about gambling. The results were published in *Social Audits: Gambling in America 1999—A Comparison of Adults and Teenagers*. Sixty-three percent of adults and 52 percent of teenagers approved of legalized gambling. Thirty-two percent of adults and 47 percent of teenagers opposed it.

Respondents (those who answered the survey) were asked about their attitudes toward the different forms of gambling. Three-quarters (74 percent) of adults and 86 percent of teenagers approved of bingo for cash prizes. Sixty-three percent of adults and 61 percent of teens approved of casino gambling, while 75 percent of adults and 82 percent of teens approved of lotteries for cash prizes. Off-track betting on horses, betting on professional sports, and playing video poker machines all received less support. (See Table 6.1.)

GAMBLING RAISES MONEY FOR STATES

The 1999 Gallup Poll asked the respondents if they agreed that legalized gambling raises money needed by states to pay for government programs and keep taxes from increasing. More than 58 percent of adults and 60 percent of teenagers said yes.

In 1998 the *Washington Post* conducted a survey for Harvard University and the Kaiser Family Foundation to find out Americans' attitudes about having legalized gambling in their own state. People were split over this issue, with 47 percent favoring legalized gambling in their state and 48 percent opposing it. Five percent had no opinion.

HOW AMERICANS GAMBLE

The 1999 Gallup Poll found that about 70 percent of adults and 26 percent of teens had done some form of legal gambling in the 12 months before the survey. In 1999, lotteries were the most popular form of gambling for adults, with 57 percent having bought state lottery tickets over the last year. Just 15 percent of teens indicated they bought lottery tickets. Bingo for money was played by 11 percent of adults (up from 9 percent in 1992 and 1996, but down from 16 percent in 1963). In 1999 a slightly higher proportion of teens (13 percent) than adults played bingo for cash. (See Table 6.2.)

Also in 1999, 31 percent of adults and only 2 percent of teens gambled at a casino in the past 12 months prior to the survey. Nine percent of adults and 5 percent of teens had wagered on

TABLE 6.1

Approval of Types of Gambling

Based on interviews conducted April-May, 1999, asking the questions: As you may know, some states legalize betting so that the state can raise revenues. Please tell me whether you approve or disapprove of each of the following types of betting as a way to help YOUR STATE raise revenue. First, do you approve or disapprove of (read A-F)? Do you approve or disapprove of it being legal?

A. BINGO FOR CASH PRIZES

	Approve %	Disapprove %	No Opinion %
ADULTS	74	24	2
TEENS	86	14	-

B. CASINO GAMBLING

	Approve %	Disapprove %	No Opinion %
ADULTS	63	36	1
TEENS	61	39	-

C. LOTTERIES FOR CASH PRIZES

	Approve %	Disapprove %	No Opinion %
ADULTS	75	24	1
TEENS	82	18	-

D. OFF-TRACK BETTING ON HORSE RACES

	Approve %	Disapprove %	No Opinion %
ADULTS	53	44	3
TEENS	55	43	2

E. BETTING ON PROFESSIONAL SPORTS, SUCH AS BASEBALL, BASKETBALL, OR FOOTBALL

	Approve %	Disapprove %	No Opinion %
ADULTS	41	57	2
TEENS	60	40	-

F. VIDEO POKER MACHINES AT LOCAL ESTABLISHMENTS

	Approve %	Disapprove %	No Opinion %
ADULTS	42	55	3
TEENS	53	46	1

Number of people interviewed = 1,523 Adults (age 18 & over) and 501 Teens (age 13-17).

Based on data from: *Social Audit: Gambling in America 1999,* The Gallup Organization, Princeton, NJ, 2000.

horse or dog races. Ten percent of adults had gambled on riverboats, compared to 1 percent of teens. (See Table 6.2.)

Sports betting is more popular among teens, with 27 percent having wagered on professional sports events in 1999, compared to 13 percent of adults. College sports attracted 18 percent of teen gamblers and 9 percent of adults. (See Table 6.2.)

A slightly larger percentage of teens (23 percent) played a video poker machine than adults (20 percent). No adults and only 2 percent of teens reported betting over the Internet for money. (See Table 6.2.)

NEW TECHNOLOGY—GAMBLING ON THE INTERNET

As seen above, Internet gambling played only a tiny role in gambling in 1999. According to the Gallup *Gambling in America 1999* poll (see above), 75 percent of adults and 66 percent of teens disapproved of Internet gambling. Most adults (76 percent) and teenagers (70 percent) believed it is easy for young people to use the Internet to gamble. They feared that easy access to Internet gambling would increase the incidence of gambling, especially among teenagers and gambling addicts.

WINNING AND LOSING—AHEAD OR BEHIND?

The 1999 Gallup researchers asked the American public if they came out ahead or behind after spending money on bets and buying lottery tickets over the past 12 months. Half (49 percent) of adults said they were behind (down from 58 percent in 1989), 26 percent said they were ahead, and 15 percent thought they broke even. Of teens surveyed, 24 percent said they were behind, 61 percent claimed they were ahead, and 10 percent said they broke even.

Does Gambling Cause Personal Problems?

The Gallup researchers asked, "Do you sometimes gamble more than you think you

TABLE 6.2

Have you gambled in the past 12 months?
Based on interviesw conducted April-May, 1999, asking the question:
Please tell me whether or not you have done any of the following things in the past 12 months. First, how about (read A-J)?

A. PLAYED BINGO FOR MONEY

	% Yes	% No
ADULTS	11	89
TEENS	13	87

B. GAMBLED AT A CASINO

	% Yes	% No
ADULTS	31	69
TEENS	2	98

C. BET ON A HORSE RACE OR DOG RACE

	% Yes	% No
ADULTS	9	91
TEENS	5	95

D. BOUGHT A STATE LOTTERY TICKET

	% Yes	% No
ADULTS	57	43
TEENS	15	85

E. BET ON A PROFESSIONAL SPORTS EVENT SUCH AS BASEBALL, BASKETBALL, FOOTBALL, OR BOXING

	% Yes	% No
ADULTS	13	87
TEENS	27	73

F. BET ON A COLLEGE SPORTS EVENT SUCH AS BASKETBALL OR FOOTBALL

	% Yes	% No
ADULTS	9	91
TEENS	18	82

G. PARTICIPATED IN AN OFFICE POOL ON THE WORLD SERIES, SUPER BOWL OR OTHER GAME

	% Yes	% No
ADULTS	25	75
TEENS	15	85

H. GAMBLED FOR MONEY ON THE INTERNET

	% Yes	% No
ADULTS	*	100
TEENS	2	98

I. PLAYED A VIDEO POKER MACHINE

	% Yes	% No
ADULTS	20	80
TEENS	23	77

J. PARTICIPATED IN RIVERBOAT GAMBLING

	% Yes	% No
ADULTS	10	90
TEENS	1	99

Number interviewed = 1004-1523 Adults (age 18 & over) and 501 Teens (age 13-17).

SOURCE: *Social Audit: Gambling in America 1999*, The Gallup Organization, Princeton, N.J. 2000.

should?" Almost twice as many teens (20 percent) as adults (11 percent) said that they did. When asked whether "gambling [has] ever been a source of problems within [their] family," almost an equal proportion of adults (9 percent) and teens (10 percent) indicated that it had. About 4 out of every 10 adults (41 percent) and nearly 3 of 10 teenagers (28 percent) reported knowing of someone outside their family for whom gambling had caused problems.

REASONS FOR AND AGAINST GAMBLING

Reasons for Favoring Gambling

In 1999 the Gallup Poll asked adults who were in favor of legalized gambling their reasons for approving of it. Thirty percent of adults believed betting is a personal freedom and if a person chooses to bet, he or she should legally be able to do so. Twenty-nine percent looked at gambling as entertainment and a way to have fun, and 18 percent considered it a good way for states to make money. (See Table 6.3.)

Of those teens who approved of legalized gambling, 30 percent thought it to be fun, 20 percent considered it a personal freedom, and 18 percent saw gambling as a way to make or win money. (See Table 6.3.)

Reasons for Opposing Gambling

The Gallup researchers asked those adults who disapproved of legalized gambling the reasons why they were against it. Twenty-five percent said wagering can ruin lives and finances, 20 percent thought betting to be addictive (habit-forming), and 16 percent saw it as cor-

TABLE 6.3

Reasons to Approve or Disapprove of Gambling

What are the one or two most important reasons why you (approve or disapprove) of legal gambling? (Based on those who approve or disapprove)

Approve of Gambling	Adults %	Approve of Gambling	Teens %	Disapprove of Gambling	Adults %	Disapprove of Gambling	Teens %
Choice/Right/Freedom	30	It's fun/enjoy/like it/entertainment	30	Ruins lives/people lose everything/ get into debt/misuse finances	25	Ruins lives/people lose everything/ get into debt/misuse finances	29
Source of state revenue/decrease taxes/provide funding	18	Choice/right/freedom	20	Addictive	20	Waste of time and/or money	14
It's fun/enjoy/like it/entertainment	29	Way to make money/win money	18	Crime/violence/corruptive	16	It's wrong/bad	12
See nothing wrong with it/harmless	8	See nothing wrong with it/harmless	14	Religious convictions	14	Addictive	10
People will gamble anyway	7	Source of state revenue/decrease taxes/provide funding	6	Causes problems for family	9	Religious convictions	9
				People in lower income or on welfare gamble	8	Don't like it	8
Way to make money/win money	6	It's legal	5				
Better to be legalized/controlled	5	Better to be legalized/controlled	2	Waste of time and/or money	7	Lose money	6
Creates jobs/brings business	4	People need to be responsible	2	Don't like it	7	Crime/violence/corruptive	5
It's legal	2	Ruins lives/people lose everything/ get into debt/misuse finances	2	It's wrong/bad	6	Causes problems for family	5
				Lose money	4	Better ways to spend money	3
I gamble	2	People will gamble anyway	1	Better ways to spend money	3	Adults only/not for children	2
Revenue benefits Native Americans	1	Creates jobs/brings business	1	Moral issues	3	Wasn't raised to gamble	2
Adults only/not for children	1	Revenue benefits Native Americans	1	Government misuses gambling revenue	2	It's fun/enjoy it/entertainment	1
People need to be responsible	1	Adults only/not for children	1	Adults only/not for children	1	People need to be responsible	1
Crime/violence/corruptive	1	Lose money	1	Wasn't raised to gamble	1	Other	11
Work in gambling industry	1	Causes problems for family	1	Way to make money/win money	1	None	3
Better ways to spend money	1	Other	7	Source of state revenue/decrease taxes/ provide funding	1	Don't know/Refused	9
Other	8	None	4	Other	13		
None	2	Don't know/Refused	10	None	1		
Don't know/Refused	2			Don't know/Refused	2		

Number interviewed = 485-964 Adults (age 18 + over) and 241-251 Teens (age 13-17).

SOURCE: *Social Adult: Gambling in America 1999*, The Gallup Organization, Princeton, NJ, 2000.

rupt and associated with crime and violence. (See Table 6.3.)

Of those teens who disapproved of legalized gambling, 29 percent said wagering can ruin lives and finances, 14 percent thought betting a waste of time and money, 12 percent believed it was wrong, and 10 percent thought it could be addictive. (See Table 6.3.)

DO OLDER AMERICANS BELIEVE GAMBLING IS BAD?

In 1998 the National Opinion Research Center (NORC) at the University of Chicago (Illinois) found that older Americans were more likely to believe that legalized gambling has bad effects on society. Over half of persons age 65 and older believed gambling has bad (31 percent) or very bad (23 percent) effects on society. In contrast, just 25 percent of the youngest group surveyed (ages 18 to 29) thought gambling has bad or very bad effects on society.

About 5 or 6 out of every 10 people (51 to 59 percent) in most of the age groups (ages 18 to 64) surveyed by the NORC agreed that legalized gambling had both good and bad effects on society. However, just 35 percent of those 65 years old and over thought so.

CHAPTER 7
GAMBLING IS A GOOD IDEA

Some of the statements have been selected from testimony before U.S. congressional committees or from debates that took place on the floor of Congress. Some words may be difficult to understand. If the editors have replaced one word with another, that word will be enclosed in brackets [ ]. If the editors feel it is important to know the word, the word will be followed by another word or words in *italics* explaining it. The definition will be enclosed in parentheses ( ).

J. TERRENCE LANNI

PREPARED STATEMENT, JUNE 1999

J. Terrence Lanni is chairman of the board and chief executive officer of MGM Grand, Inc., and a member of the National Gambling Impact Study Commission. This commission spent $5 million to conduct extensive research, traveling to cities where casinos are located and hearing the opinions of numerous local officials and residents. Lanni believes casinos are well controlled, responsible, and help the economy in poor communities. He agrees many people are addicted to gambling but points out that casinos help fund research into gambling addiction.

... [M]ost of the Commission's recommendations were either suggested or supported by the commercial casino industry, or are already being implemented by that industry today.

... [C]ommercial casinos are credited by the Commission as being a well-regulated, responsible segment of the industry.... [T]his confirms what we in the industry already know - the public has great confidence in the integrity of this form of entertainment....

... Although the gaming industry is often mistakenly viewed as a monolith *(one huge organization),* this Commission draws clear distinctions among its various segments. One of those important distinctions was the Commission's conclusion that, especially in historically impoverished *(poor),* underdeveloped communities, casinos have had a net positive economic impact. This conclusion was reinforced firsthand by the hundreds of individuals who testified before the Commission about the good jobs casinos provide.

The casino industry recognizes that, although the percentage is small, pathological *(disease-like)* gambling affects a significant number of individuals. Many of the Commission recommendations in this area were based on steps we in the commercial casino industry have already undertaken. For example, commercial casinos created the first and only foundation to date dedicated to funding research in the area of pathological gambling—the National Center for Responsible Gaming....

JEREMY D. MARGOLIS

TESTIMONY BEFORE THE HOUSE COMMITTEE ON THE JUDICIARY, SEPTEMBER 29, 1995

Jeremy Margolis is director of the Illinois State Police and was formerly an assistant United States attorney. He believes that gambling will not cause an increase in crime in the cities and states where it is legalized. He points out that many cities with gambling have lower crime rates than cities without gambling.

People often ask whether the presence of gaming in their community would cause an increase in street crime. The facts are these: Las Vegas, Nevada, the city that is synonymous *(similar)* with casinos, is among the safest cities in America. Illinois, the county's leading riverboat casino state, has experienced no increase in crime in some riverboat towns and measurable *(can be counted)* reductions in crime in others.

... Las Vegas' crime rate is significantly lower than many other tourist and convention-oriented cities, such as Miami, New Orleans, Los Angeles, Atlanta, San Diego, and San Francisco. It has a lower crime rate than college towns like Ann Arbor, Michigan, and heartland towns like Lincoln, Nebraska, and Lawrence, Kansas.

Significantly, it has a far, far lower crime rate than Orlando, Florida, the home of Mickey Mouse.

... A number of points must be made. First, comparing the demographics of problem-ridden pre-casino Atlantic City to the stable, family-oriented, economically sound, and socially responsible communities now considering casinos is like comparing night and day. Sadly, Atlantic City's problems of unemployment, drug use, extreme violence, and substandard public housing long predate the advent *(arrival)* of casinos on the Boardwalk.

... The most exhaustive *(thorough)* research on post-casino crime in Atlantic City was conducted by the noted criminologist *(a person who studies crime)* and sociologist *(a person who studies society)* Jay Albanese ("The Effect of Casino Gambling on Crime," *Federal Probation,* 39-44, 1985).... He found that the individual risk of victimization in Atlantic City was actually less than it had been before the advent of casinos, and that the crime rate for people actually present was less than it had been before visitors tripled the city's average daily population.

The Illinois experience has surpassed all expectations, and crime has, simply put, not been an issue at all.... There is no better or more accurate way to say it; crime has not been a problem.... [C]rime in the six-block area around the downtown Joliet boat decreased approximately 12 percent.

Most other Illinois riverboat towns have also reported decreases in crime.

... Probably no issue arouses more passion or poses more of a community concern than does the question of the potential involvement of organized crime in legalized gaming. Based upon a combination of history and Hollywood imagery, some people allege *(say without proof)* that organized crime will be able to infiltrate *(get in)* and exert control. Recent experience in Las Vegas and the total experience of Atlantic City and Illinois riverboats refute *(prove wrong)* this belief.

For many years, organized crime has not been a factor in Las Vegas. Aggressive and thorough regulators, and a very vigilant *(watchful of danger)* FBI (whose retired agents continue that work throughout the gaming industry), and highly efficient, tightly controlled, publicly owned companies have seen to that. In Atlantic City, organized crime never touched the casino industry.

As legalized gaming spread throughout the United States, we are seeing that those states with strong regulation and enforcement are not experiencing an influx *(flowing in)* of organized crime activity....

REPRESENTATIVE FRANK A. LOBIONDO

TESTIMONY BEFORE THE HOUSE COMMITTEE ON THE JUDICIARY, SEPTEMBER 29, 1995

Frank A. Lobiondo is a New Jersey representative to the United States House of Representatives. He thinks gambling casinos have helped the state of New Jersey by providing jobs, improving the economy, and creating tax monies. He says that crime has not increased and that gambling was the right answer for Atlantic City.

While I respect my colleagues as thoughtful people, I fear that they are motivated by stereotypes *(fixed ideas)* and misinformation of the gaming industry....

I asked to come before you today in order to tell the other side of the story....

I represent a district that includes Atlantic City, New Jersey. It was the collective decision of the people of the entire state of New Jersey to require a heavily regulated, strictly controlled casino industry to operate in one city of the state in return for making a financial commitment to the people of the state.

Atlantic City is a perfect example of how a state, with the approval of its citizenry, is the best entity to determine what, if any, type of gaming should be permitted and what conditions should be applied to that permission.

First, the law approving casinos in Atlantic City was approved by a statewide, binding referendum *(vote of the people)*. Second, the law established two state government oversight *(supervising)* agencies....

Third, Atlantic City casinos must contribute to the betterment of the state. In an age when cities and states provide tax breaks to attract new industries, Atlantic City casinos are not only subject to all state and local taxes, but must pay substantial additional taxes and fees....

Finally, New Jersey casinos directly generate 45,000 jobs, and, in fact, Atlantic City casinos provide roughly one-third of all jobs in Atlantic County. When related jobs are taken into account, another 35,000 New Jersey residents owe their employment to the gaming industry.

Gaming's opponents will tell you that Atlantic City's casinos have increased the crime rate. This is simply untrue. The visitor-adjusted crime rate, according to the WEFA group, a private consulting firm in Pennsylvania, are comparable to, and in some cases lower than, cities such as Atlanta, Nashville, and Orlando. Our crime rate nationally is far too high for my taste, but there is no indication that Atlantic City casinos have contributed to that crime rate.

Gaming's opponents will also tell you that Atlantic City's casinos have lead to economic decline in other parts of the city. The fact is that Atlantic City's economy was on the decline long before the first casino opened in 1978. If anything, Atlantic City's casinos have brought a welcome economic stability to the city.

The point to all of this is that for Atlantic City and for the state of New Jersey, casino gaming was the right answer to some serious problems. That does not mean that it is the right answer for Virginia, or Illinois, or Indiana. What is right in those states is for the residents of those states to decide. It is not for Washington to say.

WEBSTER FRANKLIN

TESTIMONY BEFORE THE HOUSE COMMITTEE ON SMALL BUSINESS, SEPTEMBER 21, 1994

Webster Franklin is the executive director of the Chamber of Commerce of Tunica County, Mississippi. He believes that legalized gambling has helped lower the unemployment rate in Tunica County by creating new jobs. He claims that gambling has improved the economy, provided more money for schools, and lowered property taxes.

Historically, Tunica County has been known as "the poorest county in the Nation...." Our community's jobs have all been based on agriculture prior to the legislation *(law)* permitting dockside gaming. Large farms, which grow cotton, soybeans, and rice, provided jobs for our citizens. But due to the mechanization *(use of machinery)* and new technology that [have] come into the farming industry, hundreds of our workers have been displaced *(put out of work)*.

Unemployment as recently as January of 1992 was as high as 26.2 percent, one of the highest in the state of Mississippi. Per capita *(per person)* income was $11,865, one of the lowest in the state. Fifty-three percent of all Tunica County residents received food stamps *(coupons from the government that people use to buy food)*. We were known for our substandard *(low-quality)* housing, poor health care delivery, and sanitation problems caused by inadequate *(not enough)* or antiquated *(old)* sewage systems.

... [S]tudies all recommended basically the same thing: Government assistance. Due to this national attention, we received much-needed government money and assistance. But that did not solve our problem—which was jobs for our citizens. It was not until the gaming industry came into our county that those jobs surfaced.

... Since the arrival of gaming, our once defunct *(no longer existing)* planning commission, now very active, has issued over $1 billion worth of building permits.

In 1993, we had 12 major casino constructions—in the construction phase. This allowed, for the first time, our citizens to go to work in the construction industry at salaries of $10 and upwards an hour. [Every] able-bodied person in the country was afforded *(given),* for the first time, the opportunity to acquire *(get)* as many overtime hours as they could withstand; therefore, they had a skill that they could take to other jobs once these facilities had been constructed.

... Nine casinos currently operate in our county, employing approximately 9,000 people. There have been more jobs in our county in 20 months than there were people.... Our unemployment rate ... was 26.2 percent.... It has gone as low as 4.9 percent. Child support collections have increased.... [T]he number of welfare recipients has decreased 42 percent. Food stamp recipients have decreased 13 percent ... and that trend continues....

Business in Tunica County is, in fact, booming.... We have new housing, RV parks, restaurants, and motels.... In fiscal year 1994, our county recorded the highest percent increase of retail sales of all of Mississippi's 82 counties, a 299 percent increase....

... This new revenue *(income)* source has allowed the county to continue the much-needed infrastructure *(schools, roads, transportation, utilities, etc. that help a community grow)* improvements.

... Revenue from gaming has allowed our county to provide an additional $1.4 million of funding for this school year. This funding will go to new classes, much-needed equipment, and increase in teacher salaries.

... Our board of supervisors also recently voted to reduce its tax on property by 32 percent.

... [G]aming has had an extremely positive impact on our local economy.

S. TIMOTHY WAPATA

PREPARED STATEMENT BEFORE THE HOUSE COMMITTEE ON SMALL BUSINESS, NOVEMBER 28, 1994

S. Timothy Wapata is the executive director of the National Indian Gaming Association. He thinks American Indian gaming helps the local business community and reduces crime. New businesses support gambling, providing jobs where none existed before. He feels that Indian gaming is helping the economy of some of the poorest counties in the United States.

Indian Gaming enterprises *(businesses)* have, by necessity, relied on and become partners with local small businesses in order to survive. Tribal Gaming enterprises are large purchasers of local business services. It has been determined that, for survival, Indian Gaming, by and large, requires partnerships with local construction and building supply firms, local restaurants, local hotels, local lounges, local cleaning firms, local clothing/uniform manufacturers, local law enforcement/security, local limousine, taxi, bus, and air transportation, local grocers and food distributors, local public utility companies, positive relationships with the local population. There is no "Wal-Mart Syndrome" *(big business taking the place of and pushing out small business)* in effect in Indian Gaming because of the reliance on the local business community to operate most Indian Gaming enterprises and because Indian Gaming creates a new type of business in a community where no business of this type existed before.

Finally, when a Tribal Gaming enterprise opens, many new small businesses are also created in order to provide necessary service to the new business. These can include restaurants, hotels, convenience stores, gas stations, banks, other entertainment ventures such as boating or skiing, childcare ventures, gaming employment training and management programs, etc. Indian Gaming enterprises are the genesis *(beginning)* for an entire support network of business ventures. Literally hundreds of new businesses nationwide have been created as a result of Indian Gaming.

Certain trends have developed in local economies with the proliferation *(growth)* of Indian Gaming enterprises. These trends are as follows:

Indian Gaming enterprises

- Stimulate and create new businesses, both Indian and non-Indian.
- Increase local economic activity, particularly increasing spending and employment.
- Reduce local public assistance rates and expenditures.
- Increase tourism and stimulate visitor spending.
- Increase federal, state, and local tax revenues.
- Result in decreased crime rates and increased local law enforcement and security expenditures.
- Result in lowered unemployment rates on the reservation and in local non-Indian communities.
- Increase Indian governmental services, economic development, and self-sufficiency.
- Nationwide, have created in excess of 100,000 direct jobs and an additional 110,000 indirect jobs, a total in excess of 210,000 jobs created as a result of the industry. These are generally jobs and work created in depressed areas *(areas weakened by slow business activity)* where no previous employment opportunity was available.

... If Indian Gaming seems an economic and social panacea *(a cure for all problems),* it is because the industry has been designed to be so.

... Indian Gaming has provided positive benefits to Indian Tribes and to the local, regional, and state areas in which the gaming is situated. This is particularly evident in counties, which the U.S. Census has identified as the poorest in the U.S. All are Indian reservations. Unemployment is as high as 80 percent, a rate similar to Third World Countries. For these areas, Indian Gaming is the only economic development tool that has worked in 200 years.

Finally, it must be remembered that gaming is an entertainment industry. People do this to have fun. The average loss at an Indian Gaming enterprise *(casino)* is less than $20. Tribes fully support, and have even created, programs to assist those who have a problem with gambling. But, the ultimate message is that people are having a good time. Their good time shouldn't be legislated out of existence *(done away with by the passing of a law).*

CHAPTER 8
GAMBLING IS NOT A GOOD IDEA

Some of the statements have been selected from testimony before U.S. congressional committees or from debates that took place on the floor of Congress. Some words may be difficult to understand. If the editors have replaced one word with another, that word will be enclosed in brackets [ ]. If the editors feel it is important to know the word, the word will be followed by another word or words in *italics* explaining it. The definition will be enclosed in parentheses ( ).

JAMES C. DOBSON

PREPARED STATEMENT, JUNE 1999

James C. Dobson is president and founder of Focus on the Family (a nonprofit organization that produces his internationally syndicated radio programs). He is also commissioner of the National Gambling Impact Study Commission (NGISC). Dobson believes that gambling destroys lives and families and preys especially on the poor, elderly, and less educated by offering them a false hope of getting rich.

The central mission of the NGISC was to study the various implications of gambling and to assess the scope of problem and pathological *(disease-like)* gambling and its effects on individuals and families. The Commission's findings, from any reasonable perspective, depict *(show)* a depth of pain and devastation in this country that compels *(forces)* a change in the way betting activity is regarded.

Clearly, gambling is a destroyer that ruins lives and wrecks families. A mountain of evidence presented to our Commission demonstrates a direct link between problem and pathological gambling and divorce, child abuse, domestic violence, bankruptcy, crime, and suicide. More than 15.4 million adults and adolescents meet the technical criteria of those disorders. That is an enormous number—greater than the largest city in this country....

One of the most scandalous features of the gambling industry, engaged in by many of our state governments, is the vigorous promotion of gambling among the poor, less-educated, and senior populations. Gambling is touted *(praised highly)* as the "ticket out of poverty," offering a last chance to riches. As such, it overtly *(openly)* preys on *(takes advantage of)* the desperation of the poor by peddling false hope.

The gambling industry pours vast sums into the campaign coffers *(funds)* of gambling-friendly politicians. It is time for the public to scrutinize *(look closely at)* those who are regularly jetted off to Las Vegas and other gambling centers to pick up these enormous contributions. We must ask, what service is being provided in return for this generosity? Republicans have been given $6.1 million and Democrats $7.6 million in recent years. During the last election in California, nearly $100 million was spent by casino interests to influence the outcome of various races and measures *(bills presented for passage as laws)*.

In summary, the illusion *(false idea)* of pain-free riches promoted by the gambling industry has been exposed.... It robs from the poor and exploits *(uses for one's own profit)* the most vulnerable *(easily hurt)*. It undermines *(weakens)* the ethic of work, sacrifice, and personal responsibility that exemplify the best qualities of American society. And if you scratch beneath the veneer *(attractive but shallow surface)* of gambling-induced prosperity, the pain, despair, and hopelessness of problem and pathological gamblers is recognized as a stark tragedy.

TOM GREY

PREPARED TESTIMONY BEFORE THE HOUSE COMMITTEE ON THE JUDICIARY, SEPTEMBER 29, 1995

Tom Grey is the executive director of the National Coalition Against Legalized Gambling. He believes that gambling will harm our economy and society. He says gambling harms other businesses, increases crime, and creates addictive gamblers.

A battle is raging across our country. Ambitious gambling promoters have been invited into our communities by some state and local officials under the guise *(appearance)* of prosperity, economic development, jobs, and a painless new source of government revenue *(income)*.

The recent, rapid spread of gambling was never the result of a popular movement. Rather, it was driven by self-interested gambling pitchmen *(promoters)* with money, high-priced lobbyists *(persons with the same interest who try to get lawmakers to vote for or against a law)*, and pie-in-the-sky *(exaggerated)* promises. Cash-starved municipalities and legislatures *(law-making bodies)*, eager for a way to increase revenue while avoiding voter backlash *(strong reaction)*, were vulnerable to the prospect of something-for-nothing.

The tide turned [against gambling] not simply because all of the major conservative Christian groups oppose the expansion of gambling, although they do. It is not simply because mainline churches—liberal, conservative, and moderate—are almost universally *(all)* opposed to more gambling, although they are. Resistance to government-sponsored gambling is growing because voters from every walk of life recognize that legalized gambling is, based on the facts, poor public policy.

... To many Americans, government's promotion of gambling is a cop-out and a double-cross. We see public officials sacrificing our communities to a predatory enterprise *(a business that takes advantage of people)*—for money. Citizens see government living off gambling profits taken from the poorest and weakest of our citizens, instead of facing up to rational choices regarding budgets and taxes.

... One could say that gambling has become the new national pastime.

... The pro-gambling initiatives *(actions)* must be stopped before our nation's economy, and its social fabric, are irreparably *(cannot be repaired)* harmed.

... The expansion of legalized gambling is a major threat to business in the United States. The gambling enterprise *(business)* cannibalizes existing businesses, stealing their customers and revenues. At the same time, gambling establishments bring new social costs that are inevitably *(surely)* paid by business.

... Pathological gamblers tend to engage in forgery *(imitating documents, works of art, or signatures in order to deceive)*, theft, embezzlement *(theft or improper use of money belonging to someone else)*, and property crimes to pay off gambling debts. They are responsible for an estimated $1.3 billion worth of insurance-related fraud (cheating) per year.

... According to a study by the Better Government Association of Chicago, "Law enforcement officials agree that the mob usually infiltrates (gets in and seizes control from within) ancillary services (services that help the gambling business) to the casinos. New Jersey law enforcement officials believe that organized crime has infiltrated legitimate businesses, such as those which provide the casinos with ancillary services including limousines, linen, meat, and vending machines."

... Increased crime costs state and local governments not only the salaries of more police officers, but prosecutors, judges, court personnel, court facilities, and prisons.

... Legalized gambling triggers (starts) the mental disorder of pathological gambling. Pathological gambling destroys the lives of thousands of Americans and devastates their families, friends, and employers. The most common argument in favor of gambling expansion is that it will yield (produce) government revenues, which can be used for programs to "help" people. But helping some people by exploiting and destroying others is bad social policy, and simply unethical.

It is important to understand that gambling addiction is just as real, and its consequences just as tragic, as alcohol or drug addiction.

... Individuals who become gambling addicts accumulate debts averaging $35,000 to $92,000 before they seek treatment, are arrested, or commit suicide. Family savings are lost, marriages end, children go unsupported. A majority of pathological gamblers turn to some form of crime to support their addiction.

... Any expansion of legalized gambling is likely to trigger thousands of new victims of gambling disorders.

JOHN WARREN KINDT

PREPARED STATEMENT BEFORE THE HOUSE COMMITTEE ON SMALL BUSINESS, SEPTEMBER 21, 1994

John Warren Kindt is a professor at the University of Illinois at Champaign-Urbana. He thinks legalized gambling adds to the problems of poor people. Businesses near gambling activities lose customers, and their workers are absent more often. He believes that gambling does not help raise money for education, as people claim it does, and that it leads to addiction among gamblers.

In recent economic history, legalized gambling activities have been directly and indirectly subsidized (paid for) by the taxpayers. The field research throughout the nation indicates that for every dollar the legalized gambling interests indicate is being contributed in taxes, it usually costs the taxpayers at least three dollars—and higher numbers have been calculated. These costs to taxpayers are reflected in (1) infrastructure costs (money spent on schools, roads, transportation, utilities, etc., that help a community grow), (2) relatively high regulatory costs, (3) expenses to the criminal justice system, and (4) large social-welfare costs.

... In the context of social-welfare issues, it is well established that legalized gambling activities act as a regressive (unfair) tax on the poor. Specifically, the legalization of various forms of gambling activities makes "poor people poorer" and can dramatically intensify many pre-existing social-welfare problems. Demographic analyses (studies of groups of people) reveal that certain disadvantaged socio-economic groups tend to gamble proportionately greater amounts of their overall income....

From the business perspective (point of view), businesses are not naive (inexperienced). With the exception of the cluster services associated with gambling, new businesses tend not to locate in areas allowing legalized gambling because of one or more of the aforementioned costs. In areas saturated *(filled)* with legalized gambling activities, pre-existing businesses face added pressures that push them toward illiquidity *(lack of cash)* and even bankruptcy.

... More subtly, traditional businesses in communities which initiate legalized gambling activities can anticipate increased personnel costs due to increased job absenteeism and declining productivity. The best blue-collar and white-collar workers, the Type-A personalities, are the most likely to become pathological gamblers.

... Legalizing various gambling activities increases the number of problems related to pathological gambling in the context of the workforce, and these costs are reflected in increased personnel costs—such as "rehabilitation costs," which can easily range from $3,000 to $20,000 (or more) per pathological gambler.

Legalized gambling activities also negatively affect education. In states with legalized gambling activities which were initiated allegedly to bolster tax revenues to "education," the funding in "real dollars" has almost uniformly decreased.

Those states which embrace legalized gambling activities can expect enormous socio-economic costs and declines in the quality of life. Unlike traditional business activities, legalized gambling activities cater to a market consisting of addicted and potentially-addicted consumers, and most pre-existing traditional businesses will find it quite difficult to compete for "consumer dollars" which are being transformed into "gambling dollars."

... Each newly created pathological gambler has been calculated to cost society between $13,200 to $52,000 per year.

... Sociologists *(people who study society)* almost uniformly report that increased gambling activities which are promoted as sociologically "acceptable" and which are made "accessible"

(available) to larger numbers of people will increase the numbers of pathological gamblers.

VALERIE C. LORENZ

PREPARED STATEMENT BEFORE THE HOUSE COMMITTEE ON SMALL BUSINESS, SEPTEMBER 21, 1994

Valerie C. Lorenz is executive director of the Compulsive Gambling Center in Baltimore, Maryland. She believes that more and more people are becoming compulsive gamblers and that this is causing crime, broken homes, increased debt, and loss of jobs.

Let me make something very clear: ALL types of gambling can become addictive, regardless of whether one gambles on or with machines, races, tickets, or games. Fortunately, only certain people will become gambling addicts. However, the number of compulsive gamblers has been increasing at an alarming rate in the past twenty years—ever since the spread of casinos and state lotteries, which has turned this country into a nation of gamblers.

... Until the mid-1970s, the typical compulsive gambler was a white, middle-aged, middle-class male. A dozen years ago, a female compulsive gambler was a rarity *(something uncommon)*. Lottery addicts were just beginning to surface. Teenage compulsive gamblers and senior citizens addicted to gambling were nonexistent.

The profile of today's compulsive gambler is truly democratic—all ages, races, religious persuasions, socio-economic levels, and education. Sixteen or sixty, the desperation and devastation is the same.

... Why? Because our governments are saying "Gambling is OK" and because gambling is now so readily available, with so very little regulation.

The formula is quite simple: availability leads to more gamblers, which leads to more compulsive gamblers. Casino gambling ... is particularly onerous *(burdensome)* because of the allure of escaping into fantasy, the fast action, and emphasis on quick money, all of which are basic factors in gambling addiction.

Gambling addiction increases socio-economic costs far greater than any amount of revenue generated for the government by the gambling industry.... Maryland's 50,000 compulsive gamblers cost the state $1.5 million per year in lost work productivity and monies that are abused [stolen, embezzled, state taxes not paid, etc.].

Other costs resulting from compulsive gambling are broken homes, physical and mental health problems, increase in social and welfare services, indebtedness, bankruptcies, and crime. Each and every one of these are far-reaching, affecting neighbors, employers, entire communities, and generations to come. These direct and indirect costs are staggering.

Taking just the issue of crime alone, virtually all compulsive gamblers, sooner or later, resort to illegal activities to support their gambling addiction. After all, money is the substance of their addiction, and when legal access to money is no longer available, these addicts will commit crimes. The crimes are typically of a nonviolent financial nature, such as fraud or embezzlement or failure to pay taxes.

While in jail, the gambling addict is neither gainfully employed nor paying federal or state taxes. The family may be surviving on drastically reduced income or be on welfare. Well-paying jobs for felons (criminals) are hard to come by, which means the gambling addict will most likely be earning less in future years, after he or she is released from prison.

... Ironically, while there are many education, prevention, and treatment programs for the substance abuser, supported by state and federal monies, what is there for the individual who becomes addicted to the government-licensed or [government-]sponsored activity, gambling? Pathetically little in a few states, nothing in most.

... The casinos historically have failed to take any measure of responsibility for compulsive gambling, and only recently have a few Indian reservations addressed this potential problem among their own people or among their customers. In short, the greed of the gambling industry is matched only by its lack of concern for its customers or the community in which it operates. That is not good business.

... First of all, it must face the fact that the problem exists, instead of continuing to ignore it or minimize it. Secondly, it must stop believing the deceptions perpetrated (brought about) by the gambling industry, that legalization of casinos or race tracks or lotteries [is] the answer to governments' fiscal (financial) woes, the answer to unemployment, or the way to stop tax increases.

... The number of compulsive gamblers in this country today runs into the millions. Who will provide the treatment, and who will pay for it? Not the gambling addicts—they have neither the money nor the health insurance....

This country can ill afford to ignore the problems caused by the proliferation (increase) of gambling and the resultant increase in compulsive gambling. We do not need the economic ruin, broken homes, and crime brought on by this industry, which encourages instant gratification, something for nothing, while making a mockery of family, work, and community.

EARL GRINOLS

TESTIMONY BEFORE THE HOUSE COMMITTEE ON SMALL BUSINESS, SEPTEMBER 21, 1994

Earl Grinols is an economics professor at the University of Illinois. He believes gambling is not like other forms of recreation, because it is harmful to society. It creates compulsive gamblers and pours money into the hands of a small group of gambling owners.

The essence of the gambling debate from an economic perspective can be understood by asking the question: Does America need another form of entertainment so badly that it is willing to add another social problem to the list that it already deals with, such as crime, alcoholism, teen pregnancy, illegal drug use, and so on?

From the federal government's perspective, a good analogy *(comparison)* might be the following: Imagine if a pharmaceutical *(drug or medicine)* company invents a new pharmaceutical. There are already other drugs available for the same purpose. The product works extremely well for 98.5 percent of the people who use it. However, for 1.5 percent of the people who use it, the drug completely ruins their life. Would the FDA [Food and Drug Administration] license this drug?

To see how gambling differs from other entertainment, we can ask, how would gambling have to be "sanitized" *(freed of undesirable qualities)* to make it like other forms of entertainment? I think at least three things are needed.

First, we would have to eliminate the 1.5 to 5 percent or so of the population who we know will become pathological or compulsive or addicted gamblers.

Second, we would have to eliminate those who gamble beyond the point of recreation or entertainment. Though gambling is a sterile transfer of money from one pocket to another, it does use time and resources. Gambling for non-recreational or non-entertainment purposes reduces national income.

Third, we would have to eliminate the massive concentration into the hands of a small group in the gambling industry of money and influence, and especially its effect on the legislative process in statehouses and city councils across America.

... Were the nation to introduce gambling everywhere, the damage would equal the costs of an additional 1990/91 recession every 8 to 15 years. This would be like the costs of an additional Hurricane Andrew, the most costly natural disaster in American history, or two Midwest floods every year in perpetuity *(forever)*.

... [Gambling draws] money away from other businesses, creating no economic development, but leaving social costs in its wake.

WORDS TO KNOW

average—the amount obtained by dividing the total by the number of units in the group. For example, the average income for families in a state is determined by adding up the income of all the families in the state and then dividing the total income by the number of families.

casino—a building or room where gambling, such as slot machines and table games (blackjack, roulette, etc.), takes place.

fix—to influence the result of a game or a race to one's advantage by offering money. For example, a person, usually a gambler, pays a player in a sporting event to change the outcome of the event. A boxer may be paid to lose a boxing match. A basketball player may be paid to score fewer points than he or she normally could.

gaming—another word for gambling; putting certain amounts of money at risk with the hope of winning more.

gross revenue—the amount of money gambling operations make after paying out winnings.

gross wager—the amount of money spent on legal gambling.

handle—the total amount of money bet at a particular gambling place. The daily handle at a racetrack is the total amount of money people bet that day.

harness racing—a form of horse racing in which the rider sits in a two-wheeled carriage, called a sulky, and directs the horse around the track. A harness racing horse may be either a trotter or a pacer (see below).

inter-track wagering (ITW)—is the showing of a race on television at a site away from the actual racetrack. The person watching may bet on the race as if he or she were at the actual track where the race is being run. In the case of ITW, the racetrack has been opened solely for the purpose of showing these televised races.

jai-alai—a very fast game in which the players use a large, curved basket strapped to the arm to catch and whip a small, hard ball against three walls and the floor of a huge playing court in much the same way as handball and racquetball are played. Originating among the Basque people in northern Spain and southern France, jai-alai means "merry festival."

lottery—a game in which the player buys a numbered ticket and hopes to win a prize if the number is drawn from among the tickets bought.

mean—an average. The mean income is the amount obtained by dividing the total income of a group by the number of people in that group. The mean income for families in a state is determined by adding up the income of all the families in the state and then dividing the total income by the number of families.

median—the number which divides the distribution into two equal parts, with half of the cases falling below this number and half being above this number. If the median household income of a state is $20,000, half the households in the state earn less than $20,000 and half earn more than $20,000.

off-track betting (OTB)—betting done on a horse or dog race without the bettor being at the racetrack. OTB bets are usually placed at a track branch office or a betting shop or parlor.

pacer—a horse used in harness racing. A pacer moves both left legs forward at the same time, then both right legs forward.

pari-mutuel—a type of betting in which gamblers bet against one another. The money wagered is put into a pool and then split among the winners.

pay-off—the amount of money left after the take-out (see below). This money is paid to the winning bettors.

place—in a horse or dog race, the horse or dog that comes in second.

quarter horse—a very swift horse that can run faster than other horses for a short distance. The name refers to the quarter-mile race the horse runs. The quarter horse runs with the rider seated in a saddle on the horse's back.

riverboat—traditionally, a large paddle-wheel boat that sails up and down the Mississippi, Missouri, and Ohio Rivers. During the nineteenth century these boats were used for moving freight and passengers. Now they are used for entertainment as floating restaurants, cruise ships, and gambling ships.

sample—a representative part of a larger whole group. In opinion polls, the people who are asked questions are the sample.

show—in a horse or dog race, the horse or dog that comes in third.

simulcast—the showing of a race on television at a site away from the actual racetrack. People then can bet on the race as if they were at the racetrack.

table games—gambling games that are normally played on a table. They include poker, roulette, craps, and blackjack.

take-out—also called the take; the percentage of the handle that is taken out by the person or company that runs the gambling activity to cover expenses.

thoroughbred—a racing horse with a heritage approved and registered by the New York Jockey Club. Thoroughbreds run with the rider seated in a saddle mounted directly on the horse's back.

trotter—a horse used in harness racing. A trotter moves the left front and right rear legs forward almost at the same time, then moves the right front and left rear legs.

wager—to make a bet; to put down money on a gambling activity. For example: *The man wagered $10 on the horse to win.* Also, the amount of a bet. For example: *The wager on the boxing match was $100.*

win—in a horse or dog race, the horse or dog that comes in first.

IMPORTANT NAMES AND ADDRESSES

American Gaming Association
555 13th St. NW
Suite 1010 East
Washington, DC 20004
(202) 637-6500
FAX (202) 637-6507
URL: http://www.americangaming.org

American Greyhound Track Operators Association
1065 NE 125 St.
Suite 219
North Miami, FL 33161-5832
(305) 871-2370
FAX (305) 893-5633
URL: http://www.agtoa.com
E-mail: agtoa@agtoa.com

American Quarter Horse Association
P. O. Box 200
Amarillo, TX 79168-0001
(806) 376-4811
FAX (806) 376-8304
URL: http://www.aqha.com

Association of Racing Commissioners International, Inc.
2343 Alexandria Drive
Suite 200
Lexington, KY 40504-3276
(859) 224-7070
FAX (859) 224-7071
URL: http://www.arci.com

Colorado Division of Gaming
720 South Colorado Blvd.
Denver, CO 80222
(303) 205-1300
FAX (303) 757-8624
URL: http://www.gaming.state.co.us

Compulsive Gambling Center, Inc.
924 East Baltimore St.
Baltimore, MD 21202-4739
HELPLINE (800) 332-0402

Council on Compulsive Gambling of New Jersey, Inc.
1315 West State St.
Trenton, NJ 08618
(609) 599-3299
HELPLINE (800)GAMBLER
FAX (609) 599-9383
URL: http://www.800gambler.org
E-mail: cgnj@800gambler.org

Gamblers Anonymous International Service Office
P.O. Box 17173
Los Angeles, CA 90017
(213) 386-8789
FAX (213) 386-0030
URL:
http://www.gamblersanonymous.org
E-mail:
somain@gamblersanonymous.org

Harrah's Casino Hotels
1023 Cherry Road
Memphis, TN 38117
(901) 762-8600
FAX (901) 762-8637
URL: http://www.harrahs.com

Illinois Gaming Board
101 West Jefferson St.
P.O. Box 19474
Springfield, IL 62794
(217) 524-0226
FAX (217) 524-0228
URL: http://www.igb.state.il.us

International Gaming and Wagering Business
888 Seventh Ave., 26th Floor
New York, NY 10106
(212) 636-2960
(800) 223-9638
FAX (212) 636-2961
URL:
http://www.gemcommunications.com
E-mail: sgibbs@gemcomm.com

Iowa Racing and Gaming Commission
Lucas State Office Building
Des Moines, IA 50319
(515) 281-7352
FAX (515) 242-6560
URL: http://www.iowaccess.org/irgc

Mississippi Gaming Commission
P.O. Box 23577
Jackson, MS 39206
(601) 351-2800
FAX (601) 351-2810
URL: http://www.msgaming.com

Missouri Gaming Commission
1616 Industrial Drive
Jefferson City, MO 65109
(573) 526-4080
FAX (573) 526-4084
URL:
http://www.dps.state.mo.us/dps/mgc/r
bfin.htm

National Association of Fundraising Ticket Manufacturers
1885 University Avenue West
St. Paul, MN 55104
(651) 603-8795
E-mail: fabian@scc.net

National Coalition Against Legalized Gambling
110 Maryland Ave. NE
Washington, DC 20002
(800) 664-2680
FAX (800) 664-2680
URL: http://www.ncalg.org
E-mail: ncalg@wavecom.net

National Council on Problem Gambling, Inc.
P.O. Box 9419
Washington, DC 20016
(410) 730-8008
HELPLINE (800) 522-4700
FAX (410) 730-0669
URL: http://www.ncpgambling.org
E-mail: ncpg@erols.com

National Indian Gaming Association
224 2nd St. SE
Washington, DC 20003
(202) 546-7711

FAX (202) 546-1755
URL: http://www.indiangaming.org

National Indian Gaming Commission
1441 L St. NW, 9th Floor
Washington, DC 20005
(202) 632-7003
FAX (202) 632-7066
URL: http://www.nigc.gov

Nevada Gaming Control Board
P. O. Box 8003
Carson City, NV 89702-8003
(775) 687-6520
FAX (775) 687-5817
URL: http://www.state.nv.us/gaming

New Jersey Casino Control Commission
Tennessee Ave. and the Boardwalk
Atlantic City, NJ 08401
(609) 441-3200
FAX (609) 441-3840
URL: http://www.state.nj.us/casinos

North American Association of State and Provincial Lotteries
2775 Bishop Rd.
Suite B
Willoughby Hills, OH 44072
(216) 241-2310
FAX (216) 241-4350
URL: http://www.naspl.org
E-mail: nasplhq@aol.com

South Dakota Commission on Gaming
118 W. Capitol Ave.
Pierre, SD 57501
(605) 773-6050
FAX (605) 773-6053
URL:
http://www.state.sd.us/dcr/gaming

U.S. Trotting Association
750 Michigan Ave.
Columbus, OH 43215
(614) 224-2291
FAX (614) 224-4575
URL: http://www.ustrotting.com

RESOURCES

The National Gambling Impact Study Commission (NGISC) was authorized by the National Gambling Impact Study Commission Act (PL 104-169; 1996) to conduct a "comprehensive legal and factual study of the social and economic implications of gambling in the United States." The study was released in June 1999. Prior to this, the most recent federal study of gambling in the United States *(Gambling in America)* was in 1976. This extensive study covers gambling from the founding fathers to 1976.

The Indian Gaming Management Staff of the Bureau of Indian Affairs (U.S. Department of the Interior) monitors tribal-state agreements and periodically releases its statistics. The National Indian Gaming Commission, a government agency, and the National Indian Gaming Association, an association of the Indian gambling industry, supply information on Indian gambling. The General Accounting Office (GAO) investigates all areas of government activity. The GAO studied Indian gaming activities in *Tax Policy: A Profile of the Indian Gaming Industry* (Washington, DC, 1997).

International Gaming and Wagering Business (IGWB), a monthly magazine about the international gambling industry, reports on every aspect of gambling. *IGWB* periodically publishes special reports on particular types of gambling activity, such as lotteries and casino gambling. Martin Christiansen and Will E. Cummings of Christiansen/Cummings Associates, Inc. (CCA), prepare an invaluable annual survey of gambling in America. The Gale Group extends its sincere appreciation to *International Gaming and Wagering Business* and CCA for permission to use selected material from their publications.

The Association of Racing Commissioners International, Inc. (Lexington, Kentucky), in its annual report, *Pari-Mutuel Racing, 1997,* summarizes statistics on horse racing, greyhound racing, and jai alai events. The Gale Group would like to thank the Association for permission to use material from its publication.

The *Greyhound Network News* is a quarterly newsletter of general information and racing news from individual states. The *Official Handbook of the American Quarter Horse Association* provides an overview of quarter horse racing in America.

The Nevada State Gaming Control Board, the New Jersey Casino Control Commission, the Colorado Division of Gaming, and the Illinois Gaming Board each publish a detailed yearly report on casino gambling in their states. The South Dakota Commission on Gaming, the Missouri Gaming Commission, the Mississippi Gaming Commission, and the Iowa Racing and Gaming Commission also produce annual statewide reports on casino gambling.

The Gale Group expresses its sincere appreciation to the Gallup Organization (Princeton, New Jersey) for permission to use its survey *Social Audits: Gambling in America 1999—A Comparison of Adults and Teenagers (1999).*

The American Gaming Association (AGA; Washington, DC), an industry trade group, published the first annual *State of the States: The AGA Survey of Casino Entertainment* in 1999. The AGA survey of casino gambling and entertainment provided information collected by a number of sources that polled more than 80,000 people.

INDEX